MY MEMORIES WITH LIFE

THE BOOK COVERS MEMORIES IN VARIOUS LIFE SPAN INCLUDING
WORKING IN STATE BANK OF INDIA FOR 39 YEARS

VIJAY SWAROOP JAIN

प.पू. निमित्तज्ञानी आचार्य १०८
श्री विमलसागरजी महाराज

Gurudev Acharya Shri 108 Shri Vimal Sagar ji Maharaj !

Gurudev's blessings!

Vatsalya Ratnakar, Charitra Chakraborty Acharya Guruvar Shree 108 Shri Vimal Sagar Ji Maharaj!

Avataran (Birth)- Ashwini Krishna Saptami--1st January 1915

in Village-Kosma (District-Etah-Uttar Pradesh-Bharat) !

Samadhi - 29 December 1994 at Parasnath (Shri Sammed Shikharji- Jharkhand Pradesh-Bharat) !

During the period of Sadhutva - performed many fasts including 1234 fasting of character purification fast, 1008 fasting of Jin Sahasranam fast and 720 fasting of three Chaubisi fast!

Gave initiations to - 40 Muni , 24 Aryika , 1 elak , 21 chhullak and 17 chhullika !

ॐ ह्रीं श्रीं क्लीं ऐं बड़े बाबा अर्हं नमः स्वाहा:
श्रीमद् आचार्य देव श्री 108 विद्यासागर जी यतिराज
निर्यापक मुनि पुंगव श्री 108 सुधासागर जी महाराज

Acharya Guruvar Shree 108 Shri Vidya Sagar Ji Maharaj ,Muni Pungav Shri 108 Shri Sudha Sagar ji !

Humble Regards,
to
Acharya Guruvar Shree 108 Shri Vimal Sagar Ji Maharaj !Acharya Guruvar Shree 108 Shri Vidya Sagar Ji Maharaj ! Muni Pungav Shri 108 Shri Sudha Sagar ji Maharaj !
Who are GOD GIFTs for me like Chintamani Ratns (gems),
THEIR blessings have always been with me and will remain ever !
and to
My Mother Smt. Mahadevi Jain (Late) and
Father Shri Har Prasad Ji Jain (Late) !

Whose memories are remaining .

With Bowing my head in their feets ,
Vijay Swaroop Jain
"Saubhagy" 118, Manas Nagar, Shahganj, Agra - 282010 (Uttar Pradesh - BHARAT-India)
Contact : 9319773237 , 6397407367
email : vijaysjain999@gmail.com

Contents

Foreword

19 July 2000 !

I am 50 years old today !

For the past several days, this idea was going on that various aspects of my life, like ups and downs, happiness-sadness, coincidence-disconnection etc. should be given shape in the form of articles. I am starting this work from today. Let us see how long and how much This work will be completed.

While the memories of the early days of life shake on one hand, on the other hand it also gives comfort that no one can avoid happening and happiness-sadness, coincidence-disconnection. Everything is planned / controlled according to karma.

And here the karmic principle of Jainism appears to be accurate where it is clear that you will have to bear the fruits of your actions and no God, gods, king, parents, siblings, relatives will/can not become a participant in the fruits of the karma.

Vijay Swaroop Jain

"Saubhagy", 118, Manas Nagar, Shahganj, Agra - 282010 (Uttar Pradesh - Bharat-India)

Contact : 9319773237 , 6397407367

email :vijaysjain999@gmail.com

Preface

-Like bank interest, life also went on increasing in the form of nights and days and remained unaware when the age of 70 yrs reached .

-Death of both parents in 5 days when I was aged seven - eight years.

-Compelled to live with relatives as there was no alternate.

-Blessings of elder brother Mr. Bhagwan Swaroop Jain and sister-in-law Mrs. Jinendra Kumari Jain to get education and job in State Bank of India .

-Marriage, Children's screams , their education - marriages as well as mental and financial problems ,couldn't let me know how far have reached while battling ?

-At the age of 50, remembered how life was lived and in the midst of ups and downs, sweet &sour experiences , deceivings and neglectful behavior from family/acquaintances/companions (this is destiny)!

Arghya is offered only to the rising sun. The drowning is only given farewell !

-After giving full support (mental, financial and emotional) by beloved wife (Mrs.) Sushma Jain for 49 years left for her heavenly abode On 23 February 2020 leaving me alone,at the crucial time of my life, when her support was amust to live.

-The idea of storing such different experiences and events is the reason for the emergence of this book !

On my 50th birthday (19-07-2000) I was in Jaipur for bank work,where my second daughter, (Mrs.) Neetu Jain lives, who is currently teaching at Anselm's College, North City, Jaipur.

The writing of this book started from Jaipur.

Vijay swaroop Jain

"Saubhagy", 118, Manas Nagar, Shahganj, Agra - 282010 (Uttar Pradesh - Bharat-India)

Respected Bhai Saheb,Bhabhi ji and Sushma ji with family !

CHAPTER ONE

Journey to Life !

Beginning of life!

Actual date and time of birth is unknown but my date of birth as per educational certificates is 19th July 1950.

According to the information received from the eldest sister, Late Smt. Chandraprabha Jain, my birth is on Ashwin Krishna Ekadashi and the place of birth is Agra. That day was the day of Ram Barat procession in Agra.

The memories I have in my mind, are from around 4-5 years age.

I remember village-Usayani (Distt.Firozabad) while expanding the shop, used to talk about the tables along with keeping things with father. Some incidents before that are alive in my memory like going to temple in the morning (this sequence remains continue even in rainy season) .In the absence of an umbrella had to go to the temple using a sack of sackcloth. No family member got anything to eat prior to worship at temple.

At that time Bhai Saheb Shri Bhagwan Swaroop Jain was studying in Agra Hostel. May be completing his M.A.(English) or L.T. I also remember that when Bhai Saheb used to go to the village, father used to keep ghee and pedas(sweets) with him while returning.

It is also remembered that the time of night, sometimes on foot and sometimes sitting on the back and shoulders of the father, I used to come and go to the temple. Once when I was on his shoulders Bhai Saheb asked father to get me walk onfoot.

At that time there would have been so much intelligence that on whose shoulders I am going to the temple, he himself is the form of God.

I remember many incidents related to father Shri Har Prasad Jain, while no specific incident related to mother Shrimati Mahadevi Jain is there ,except one that when she received message of her brother's death , she cried badly and had hurt his head with a lota.

Father used to run "General Merchant-cum-Sweets Shop" which was situated at Village-Usayani on Tundla Firozabad Main Road, and the house was behind the shop. Because the shop was on the road, all the visitors who used to stop there. go after eating and drinking water.

This facility was available free of cost to relatives.

Various items were put in the shop in the morning and kept inside while closing the shop in the evening. I also used to sit at the shop along with my father. The main product of the shop was Khoye ka peda (a sweet dish) which was of one pav (about two hundred fifty grams). On the top there was a symbol of Chhatanki (Chhatanki - a weight ,used to weigh at that time , of about 60 grams).

Father was also a Vaidya, but he did not make this qualification a source of income, otherwise the condition of our family would not have been as pathetic as it was after his death.

I remember that sometimes in the middle of the night, on receiving information about patients from the nearby villages , without paying attention to the time, he used to hang lanterns on stick and go out to see the patients.

The cause of father's death was probably a loss in business. Because he, in addition to the shop, started a stuffing business (wheat and gram), and that's when he lost.

It was the result of the education given to me by my father at home , that when I was admitted in the first class, I sat in the first class only for 1 day.

On the second day the Head Master Saheb (who was a Maulvi Sahib and used to wear round glasses, his face is light, he used to have a black beard) said to the father that I was already aware of first and second class courses and he directly enrolled me in third class.

The school was in front of the shop, across the road, and on my admission, all the staff were given pedas(sweets).

I have in mind pictures of some people belonging to the village. There was a Tau from Isauli. He was very affectionate and I would get peanuts when went to his shop. There is another person whose name I can't remember but people used to call him dumb because he couldn't speak/hear properly.

A few days after my birth, when my parents were with me in Agra, there was a robbery in our house in the village and the robbers took away all the belongings of the house. On opposing by my elder brother ,he was slapped by the robber.

This incident happened due to a small lapse in the security system. Dad used to sleep with the lock locked from inside. But that day the neighbor uncle Adal singh slept with brother , he had only latched and the dacoit had break a little walland entered a child inside, who opened the latch and all the dacoits entered inside.This incident had a major impact on my elder brother ,who throughout his life used to sleep only after making sure that the locks were installed in the house.

The younger sister narrated an incident that at that time she was a child and did not know anything about what robbery was. When father came from Agra, he childishly said, "Dadaji" (father was called Dada ji) there has been a robbery here, have you brought something to eat for us? Hearing this, everyone smiled even in times of sorrow.

As a child, my boils used to come out a lot and my father used to take me to Tundla to consult Dr. Ghosh. Father had a lot of cycling practice and often used to travel from village to Agra by cycle to purchase goods for selling at the shop.One more incident,I remembered that the younger sister was ill and Mosambi(fruit) were purchased for her, to extract the juice of Mossami. One day after washing my mouth, it seemed that there was blood in my nose. When father learnt this he ordered me to start eating musammi, while later it was known that the color of the medicine applied in the eyes was.

After entering the school, the time of about 1 year was fine. In the meantime, the search for a wife for Bhai Saheb started and his relationship with Mrs. Jinendra Kumari Jain, daughter of Mr. Jagdish Prasad Jain of Awagarh, was fixed. The ceremony of seeing her took place in Tundla by Shri Vasudev Prasad Jain, who used to be the maternal uncle of our mother and also the maternal uncle of sister-in-law. I also remembered Jain Fare at FIROZABAD where we were staying in tent , sister-in-law was called. There were tents in the Jain fair and the passengers used to stay in those tents.

Due to loss in business, my father became sick and took bed.

I had a distaste for milk since childhood. After many attempts, my parents were unable to feed milk , so they came up with a new trick. They started feeding me semolina from boiling milk used to prepare khoya.

My maternal uncle, Shri Sukhdev Jain, resident of Pilkhat, used to live in Awagarh .Cousin of my maternal uncle Shri Moolchand Jain also living with Mama ji (Shri Sukhdev Jain)and used to do confectionery/sweets work jointly. After death of Shri Sukhdev Jain the entire work was taken over by Shri Moolchand Jain. After the death of Shri Moolchand Jain, my father brought Mrs. Indravati Jain (wife of Shri Moolchand Jain) to our home at the village . She had two sons Prakash Chandra Jain and Umesh Chandra

Jain. Mama Ji died before the birth of Umesh Chand Jain. Umesh was born in the village itself. Even after that, maternal aunt and children stayed at our house in the village. At the time of father's illness, maternal aunt had gone to Awagarh along with the children.

The incident at the time of my father's death is still alive before my eyes. How he was brought down from the upper storey (atta) where he died and his body was placed in the courtyard.

Mother probably had a disease of TV (Tubeculosis), which was not curable at that time. Its genetic effect also happened to two sisters Mrs. Maina Devi Jain and Mrs. Ratan Prabha Jain and both were treated at TV Hospital in Agra (formerly called American Hospital). It took a long time and both got cured. I remembered that Mrs. Mainadevi Jain used to come every month by train from Etawah and she was given "Rail Travel Concession Pass" every month by the government. Younger sister also used to come to Agra for treatment.

Father died on Kartik Krishna Panchami in the morning of 1958 and mother died 5 days later on Kartik Krishna Dashami.

It was also a surprise. I was seeing men and women weeping, but I was not crying and was silent. This was also said by the mother. That scene is still alive in my attention.

After the death of my father, I was ill for about 15 days. I had a intermittent fever and in the same fever, my right eye's vision was greatly reduced and now there is no way to cure it.

After the death of mother and father, brother-in-law of Etawah, Shri Raj Bahadur Ji Jain stayed in the village and continued the shop.

I remember an incident from that time. Sister, MainaDevi Jain, was afraid of rats. One day, brother-in-law caught a mouse and put it in the pocket of the jacket, and asked Jiji to withdraw some money from the jacket. She put her hand, but nothing happened because the mouse had gone out due to a hole in the pocket.

Because of non profit from the shop, brother-in-law returned to Etawah after a few months.

Father had taken loan from some people. Those people used to come for repayment. After father's death, pressure was built on Elder brother. Some of them are Shri Satya Ram (from any other village), Shri Srinivas Jain, Shri Amritlal Jain (who has our ancestral house).

Bhai Saheb's father-in-law, Shri Jagdish Prasad Jain, along with his friend Shri Chandra Prakash Jain, who seemed to be our brother-in-law, came to the village with a truck and loaded all the goods and kept it at Tundla in the house of Shri Vasudev Prasad Ji and took our family to Awagarh. I remember this incident that when we were coming from village to Tundla by Ikka (a trasport vehicle being run by horse) to Tundla, Shri Amrit lal Jain, whom we used to call uncle, took brother's cycle, in lieu of his money lent to father.By this instance I realised that since beginning, the importance of money was more than friendship and family relations at that time and today it has become even more important.

Memories of Awagarh !

After this, I and my sister Ratan prabha Jain stayed with our sister-in-law in Awagarh at her house. I enrolled there in the fourth class. Due to adverse circumstances, I could not study and failed.My

sister got married with the help of Shahji Shri Jagdish ji Jain. At the time of their marriage, the sister's foot was burnt.

In Awagarh, brother of sister-in-law, Mr. Vinay Kumar Jain was in the fourth class with me. Two sons of Mr. Chandra Prakash Jain, Pramod Kumar Jain, Rajesh Kumar Jain and also Prabhu Dayal Jain studied with me.

Bhabhi ji's Baba Lala Phool chand Jain , Sarraf (Jwellers) was a very religious person. A lot was learnt from him and got influenced. Many times he got the shop closed for upto six months and performed long journeys to pilgrimages. His father (Bhabhi ji's par Baba) had been a court inspector under the British rule.

Lalaji had 2 sons. Mr. Jagdish Prasad Jain and Mr. Naresh Chand Jain. Mr. Jagdish Prasad Jain was a cloth merchant at Awagarh and Mr. Naresh Chand Jain was an advocate in Agra. The relationship between the two brothers was not very cordial. I, initially saw the robust nature of Lala Phool chand jain ji, it gradually faded with age and remained in pathetic condition in the last. There was some opposition with the elder son Shri Jagdish Prasad Jain and Shri Jagdish Prasad Jain along with the family moved to another house on rent. But later his aunt of Badnagar called back after persuasion. At that time I was in Awagarh. I remembered that younger sister of sister-in-law, whose name was Rajesh Jain, used to study in the seventh class in Awagarh. While playing, she was hit by an iron ball in her head. Considering a minor injury, the upper treatment was done, but the injury kept increasing inside and eventually took her. She was admitted to Agra Emergency, where she died. I remember when her dead body was taken by a matador to Awagarh . This incident affected his father ,particularly who could not return to normal for a long time.

Sister-in-law's father Shri Jagdish Prasad Jain was also a religious person like his father. He also used to stage various religious plays(dramas). In 1986, he got performed Panchkalyanak, under tue guidance of Nimittgyani Acharya Shree 108Shri Vimalsagar Ji Maharaj, in the big temple of Awagarhand got the idol of Lord 1008 Shri Bahubali Swami ji installed. At the same time, according to the instructions of Acharya Shree, I also decided for an idol of Lord 1008 Shri Parshvanathji ,which was taken on Sunday, 7.12.1986, whose sacrifice amount was Rs 451, citation writing Rs 11 and Matraka Yantra Rs 41. I was told by Acharya shree to get small temple built on first floor , in my house 4 mini MIG ,Friends Colony ,Shahganj , Agra.But nothing could be done and the Lord is seated in the "Shri Vardhaman Nagar Temple in Shahganj Agra.

Arrival in Agra !

In the month of July 1960, Bhai Saheb took us to Agra and started living in a rented house at Pul Chinga Modi, Loha Mandi, Agra. Shri Kusum Chand Jain also lived in the same house and we used to call his mother as Phula jiji. There was a relationship between the two families ,that I don't remember.

And thus I returned to my birth place .

At the time of coming to Agra in the year 1960, Bhai Saheb was working as English teacher in Ratn Muni Jain Inter College, Loha Mandi, Agra, and the salary was only Rs.60 per month.

I was also admitted in class 6 in the same school. After a day or two of admission, there was a test of English. I had never studied English in the past, so there was no question of getting pass the test. However,due to special emphasis by Bhai Saheb and keen interest by me, I got 82% marks in English in the examination.In Science, Geography, Mathematics, I was not too briliant but kept passing.

First daughter of Bhai Saheb, Sunita was born in the year 1961 (2 September 1961).

Sister-in-law's father, Shri Jagdish Prasad Jain, used to have a lot of support. Sometimes he used to send goods from Awagarh.

After about a year, Bhai Saheb's job got terminated from Ratn Muni Jain Inter College and he got job in Shri Mahavir Digambar Jain Inter College Hari Parvat, Agra with the help of Shri Mahendra ji (Sahitya Bhavan M G Road Agra).

Bhai Saheb told that earlier Acharya Shri 108 Shri Vimal Sagar ji Maharaj forecasted that your job is about to go and also said that don't worry, another job is ready.

The words of Acharya Shree were to be true and I bowed down to the feets of Acharya Shree.

I was also got admitted to VII th class in MD Jain College (Shri Mahavir Digambar Jain Inter College, Hari Parvat, Agra) and studied there, till class 12th.

There is a Jain temple in the college. Shree1008 Shri Bhagwan Shantinath ji ,ancient idol and idols of other Tirthankars are there in the temple. And now that temple has become even more beautiful and worth seeing. There is a huge Manstambh outside the temple.

At that time Shri Bal Krishna Das Baijal was the Principal. He was a very capable and strict administrator.

In college, I was not very fast at studies. Although my brother's fellow teachers ,sometimes praised my ability. I remember a few incidents of seventh and eighth class. I was accompanied by the son of the temple gardener. He was brilliant in studies even with limited resources.

Because Bhai Saheb had to stay even after college time, so I used to read books /magazine/ newspapers sitting in the college library and this increased my knowledge a lot. Along with this, I also had a passion for reading and that hobby fulfilled here. I remember Some memories of Bhai Saheb's teaching period which he told . One of his colleagues ,whose name I don't remember but his nick name was LADDO GOPAL, wrote an application for fee waiver of his brother-in-law. He wrote in Hindi and described Brother-in-law as "KANOONI BHAI"(Hindi traslation of brother-in-law). When this application reached the management, they asked what "KANOONI BHAI" meant. He gave reply that I have translated Brother-in-Law in Hindi as "KANOONI BHAI". Everyone started smiling and his fee waiver was approved.

When I was giving the high school examination, the principal's signature was not on the admit card and I was told from the examination center to get it signed tomorrow, otherwise I will not be allowed to sit in the examination. Bhai Saheb took me to the house of Pricipal Mr. Baijal sahib on his bicycle. I got his signature done on the admit card. I noticed that Mr. Baijal sahib had a dog who was standing next to him. I playfully put my hand on the dog. When I put it, it started barking very loudly. Mr. Baijal sahib calmed him down.

From Pul Chinga Modi's house, we stayed in a house in Kinari Bazar, just above the path of barry shoes remained there only for few months .Fro there we shifted to Chhipitola in the house of Dr Girish Chand Kotia . There were many tenants in this house. In the upper floor, Mr. Kapoor Chand lived with his family. He had a business of disposal goods. Downstairs lived a Jain family whose head was called Munimji. Munimji died during our stay thereat. There was a family living in a room in a corner which used to sell gajak etc.

Doctor Sahab used to live outside and his wife used to live in the same house. Due to lack of electricity in the house, there was inconvenience and we used to study under the light of lamps.

Two sisters of sister-in-law(Bhabhi ji) were born in this house.

In summer, beds were sprinkled on the roof and they used to study in lamps lights. After several efforts, electricity connection was arranged .

In class IX, i was in IX B section. I remember the names of the teachers , Mr. Upadhyay ji (taught Geography), Mr. RS Aggarwal (taught Hindi), Mr. Babulal ji (taught Mathematics).

NCC parade is also taken care of. Shri Bhartiya ji was in charge of it, who used to be in the lead role in the morning prayer meeting and his loud voice used to cause pin drop silence in the whole field. Later I joined NCC (Air Wing)) in which models of aeroplanes were made and Mr. Lavania ji was in charge of it. Bread butter was disrtributed after the parade.

A prayer was spoken in the prayer meeting, some lines of which are as follows:

Hai shaantinaath bhagavan ! tujhe namoo main !

araham namoo ,jin namoo, bhagavan namoo main !

(Oh Lord Shantinath! I bow to you !

I bow to Arham ,I bow to Jin , I bow to God !)

In the year 1964, we left Chhipitola and shifted to Mr. Bengali Mal Jain's house in Raja Mandi. Mr. Bengali Mal had 4 sons and one daughter. Mr. Satish Jain, Sumat Prakash, Ajay and Abhinandan. A hall in the same house was also taken on rent by Shri Arvind, Pramod, Rajesh sons of Shri Chandra Prakash Jain,

Awagarh. Bhabhi ji's brother Shri Ashok Kumar Jain, Vinay Kumar, Harsh Kumar also lived here together. Food for all the people was cooked by Bhabhi ji Smt. Jinendra Kumari Jain . I now realize that even though there was no facility at that time, sister-in-law used to cook the food of so many people ,alone. Nowadays, even after having all the facilities, a maid is also employed for the work of a single family of few members.

In the year 1963, Shri Ashok Kumar Jain's son Shri Jagdish Prasad Jain was married from village Lalpur near Awagarh. In the marriage he got a kodak camera and a philips transistor which was taken by him to someone's marriage from where both things were taken away by some person.

Mr. Ashok Kumar Jain was completing his LLB (Final) in 1966 and got a job in State Bank of India on 8 October 1966. In the year 1967, Mr. Ashok Kumar Jain was in the upper house of Badri Das Bankelal cloth merchants in Raja Mandi.

Vinay Kumar, Pramod Kumar , Rajesh Kumar Jain and Shrikant (who is the son of a doctor in Awagarh) studied with me in high school, but these people could not pass and returned to Awagarh.

I got a scholarship after passing class 10th (UP Board's high school examination) with good marks. I bought a cycle from that money in the year 1966. We used to go to tuitions with the same cycle.

I and Vinay Kumar passed out and admitted to class XI. There is some rememberance of classes XI, XII. Among teachers Mr. Lavania Sahab, who lived in Gandhinagar, used to teach chemistry and we also took tutions from him (I and Vinay Kumar used to go to tuitions on separate cycles). Once my cycle collided with Vinay Kumar and both of us got minor injuries) . Mr.Goswami ji taught Maths ,when he used to clean the black board with duster, his other hand also moved at the same speed.

I remember an incident of Twelfth class (XII) that a fellow who was smart in studies and Lavania Sahib had special attention on him, did everything wrong in the practical of chemistry. When Lavania Sahib came to know about this, he took care of him by providing detailed information to the examiner about him and got maximum marks in practical.

After intermediate in the year 1967 I took admission in B.Sc in Agra College and Vinay Kumar Jain took admission in Dayalbagh for Electrical Diploma. Although I wanted to go in engineering but could not go due to family circumstances, mainly financial condition.

In Agra College, Physics was taught by Mr. HP Singh and Mathematics by Mr. S S Seth, I am not recollecting the name of Professor of Chemistry.

Dr. Manohar Ray was the Principal at that time. Once I read on the notice board that there is a debate competition. I got prepared a complete speech on the topic of debate in English with the help of Bhai Saheb.

I directly reached to the Principal Dr. Manohar Ray and requested for participating in the debate. Only then it came to know that I cannot participate in the debate directly. According to some rules, the team is selected for the debate and the same can participate in the debate. The team participating in the debate had already been selected, so my preparation was in vain.

There was some lack in studies in the second year of B.Sc and I got supplementary in Chemistry which also could not be successful and as such my BSc was completed in 3 years.

Keeping in mind the plan of any work / job after B.Sc., I took admission in MSc (Maths) in RBS College in 1970. The MSc class were from 7:00 to 10:00 in the morning and after 10:00 I remained free for any work/job.Though I did not get any job while studying in M.Sc. but got tuitions to some St peters School Children by going to their homes.Apart from this, in house 26/67, Ahir Pada, we started tution batches along with brother, in which English was taught by brother and science and maths by me .

After doing MSc (Previus) in the year 1971, I took admission in MSc (Final). I had been wishing to live in my own house from the beginning but this could not be possible due to low income. In the year 1975, in conversation with Mr. R. D. Sharma, who was with me in the bank, I found out that Mr. Rajendra Sharma , who was in Railways and posted at Agra Cantt with Mr. R. D. Sharma's father, is developing a colony. He fixed my meeting with Mr. Rajendra Sharma ji who lived in Saket Colony.

And finally in 1975 I deposited an amount of 1500 rupees for a plot of 200 yards in his proposed "Manas Nagar" colony. The name of society was "Prempuri Co-operative Housing Society Ltd., at the address of 8/249, Bhogipura, Shahganj Agra, which was later changed to 70, COD Colony, Agra.Secretary of the society was Sri Ram ji lal who was a post master.

A few days later a junior engineer of ADA (AGRA DEVELOPMENT AUTHORITY) met and told that ADA approval for Manas Nagar has not been given.I rushed to Shri Rajendra Sharma who politely said you have some faith on me otherwise take your money back. Agreeing with his words, I decided not to take the money back and this decision was absolutely right because I was allotted a plot in Manas Nagar and got a house built.

After this, in the year 1978, ADA took out an advertisement for the houses built in Shahganj, Agra. Rs.4000 was to be deposited but money was not available. At this stage my friend Shri Santosh Kumar Gupta come forward to help me .Shri Gupta ji used to live in Freeganj with his elder sister . He,with the consent of his sister took a loan of ₹ 4000 on his FDR and gave it to me which was deposited in ADA on 31/3/1978, the last day of the scheme.

Shri Santosh Gupta and Smt. Reeta Gupta !

The future statement of Nimittgyani Acharyas hree 108 Shri Vimal Sagar Ji Maharaj !

In the year 1978, Acharya Shri had come to Agra and stayed at Belanganj, Kachoda Bazar Dharamshala. He used to solve the problems of the public from 1:30 PM to 2:30 PM daily. I reached him on a day and asked him about my own house. Without asking any further, he told from his own knowledge that you have invested money in two places and both the places will be of disputes in future. I got surprised and came bach home.Howeveron the next day I again approached him and asked for get the deposits back ,for which

He refused.In next pages you will read how his prophecy ,made 30 years ago, came true.

The house was allotted to me in May 1979.

The credit for getting this house goes to Mr. Santosh Kumar Gupta.

A FRIEND IN NEED IS A FRIEND INDEED !

In this way everyone in the family was happy after getting the house. House No. 4 Mini MIG, Friends Colony, Shahganj, Agra was allotted. Sushma, my wife , was extremly happy.

To get the repairing / renovation work done in Friends Colony house, masons etc were employed and I remember that I used to drop Sushma here before going to the bank to look after the work and bring her back after returning from the bank in the evening.

Later for a few days my friend Mr. RC Sharma, who was with me in the bank, used this house for his residence as his house nearby (B-79, New Shahganj) was getting completed.

On 2 February 1980, Mr. SK Gupta married Mrs. Rita Gupta in Lakhimpur (which is his native village). To attend their wedding, I, Sushma, Neeru, Neetu reached their village by train and attended the wedding. Theremy family got Gupta's parents' love and affection. Lived like family members. I remember an incident from that time. We went to visit Nepal by short cut and returned with some clothes etc. The next day Umesh and some friends also went there and while returning, some anti-social elements got their luggage kept in the name of checking and they returned empty handed.

When we decided to come to 4, Mini MIG Friends Colony from AhirPada, then sister-in-law (Bhabhi ji) said that at later date you may refuse to disallow them. On being asked like this, I replied that the house is yours. Though it is in my name, everyone will live together and on such assurance everyone was happy. In January/February 1980, we shifted to this house with Bhai Saheb, Bhabhi ji , Myself,Sushma,Sunita, Vineeta Praneeta, Sukirta, Pankaj, Neeraj, Neeru, Neetu .

On 20.02.1980 Grah Pravesh(Entering to New House) program was celebrated, with which Bhai Saheb's first book "Naunihal Gayan" was released by Dr. Rajeshwar Prasad Chaturvedi, Principal Degree College, Shikohabad.

When shifting after vacating Ahir Pada's house, along with the happiness of own house, there was also the pain of leaving the company of old companions and at that time I and Mataji (Land lady--Mrs. Hazarilal Mittal) wept a lot.

After shifting to the colony the idea of starting a convent school was formed because the colony was new,. We were just thinking that one of our friend Mr. Vinod Bansal (who was with us in MSc) alongwith another friend Rajkumar Kulshrestha and Said we have opened a school in the name of "Milton Public School" in Friends Colony and cooperate for the children in it. In such a situation, the idea of opening our school had to be droped and all the children of our house were also admitted to Milton Public School. At that time the principal of the school was Mrs. Chitra Kulshrestha, (wife of Mr. Rajkumar).

In the year 1982, the foundation stone of Manas Nagar house was laid on 20th September at 8:00 AM and the construction work started. At that time the contract of the house was given to Shri Banwari Lal Contractor. He took a shovel from the worker and threw it. When the news came to me, I went and talked to him, he told that this land is ours. I calmly assured him that we have bought this land from the society and if you will prove it That's yours, we'll leave. He's gone and never came back again.

Acharya Shree's controversial statement was in this context, it cannot be said that the electrical work was done by Gautam Bijliwala and the sanitary work was done by Trilokchand (Triloki). It used to come. At that time the price of bricks was Rs 320/355 per thousand. 3000 brick truck used to come to about 1065. The iron frame of the door used to come for about one hundred rupees.

In the year 1985-86, this house was leased to State Bank of India and Mr. Mahesh Chand Sharma, who is my friend, lived with his family. This house was vacated from the bank on 31st March 1987.

In the year 1984, I stayed alone in Shikohabad for some time with Sushma's aunt Mrs. Kusum Lata Jain and later moved the family to Shikohabad. The first house was in front of the house of elder sister Mrs. Chandraprabha Jain, upstairs in a Pandit ji's house. The advantage of staying there was that the Jain temple was nearby and the whole family used to have food only after having darshan. There was a very domestic relationship with the family. Vivek was very young, he used to touch Saxena's mother's feet daily and get blessings. Saxena's children Jeenu, Gunjan and Chintu were very shaken by Sushma and all the children used to play together. Later Saxena's family also stayed in Agra and then finally shifted to Ghaziabad. Meetings became very less. We went to Jeenu's wedding. Saxena Sahab passed away in 2020.

When the problem of drinking water in this house increased a lot, I saw another house which belonged to a Doctor Saheb (Dr. Kapoor) and was on the top floor in Katra Bazar. Lived in the house of a teacher. I bought my first car Maruti 800 while living in this house.

When I was taking the family to Shikohabad, Bhai Saheb Shri Bhagwan Swaroop ji brought the manuscripts of all the books (poems) he had written and started showing Sushma that I have not wasted my time and have written so much. In the same way, it was sad to leave the family, hearing these words brought tears to my eyes.

There is a lot of work of Desi Ghee in Shikohabad and most of the establishments are of Jain people. From here Desi Ghee goes to Calcutta by trucks. At that time the rate was around ₹ 50 / ₹ 52 per kg. At that time payment used to come by draft. And huge amount of drafts used to come in the name of these people's labor. Once in the main branch in Shikohabad when I saw a check for payment of huge amount, I called the person concerned in front of me. When he was asked how much If payment is there, he could not tell anything and said Seth ji knows. Later many such accounts were found in which big transactions were taking place. It was impossible to completely control such accounts, yet efforts were made to keep the accounts regular. and belong to the right persons.

Mr. Surendra Kumar Jain used to take desi ghee for his house from here and had a very good relationship with him. After his passing, his son Mr. Anil Kumar Jain handled the business well and is still doing it.

In Shikohabad, one son of elder sister was married in 1982 and the second son was married in 1990.

In the year 1997, there was the marriage of Mr. Sharad Luthra (friend of Neeraj) on November 23 and Pragati Nagar, daughter of my friend Mr. Anil Nagar on November 24, 1997.

Death of eldest sister Mrs. Chandra prabha jain !

2 December 2000 !

In Jhunjhunu, where I was posted in those days, at about 9:30 PM information was received that, in Shikohabad, eldest sister Mrs. Chandraprabha Jain, has passed away at 7:00 PM . Immediately after giving charge to another officer, rushed toDelhi by Shekhawati Express train. Reached Delhi at about 5:45 AM on 3rd December 2000. Rushed to Agra from Delhi by Taj Express and went to Shikohabad with Umesh .

Death of elder sister Mrs. Ratan prabha jain !

31 October 2021 Sunday!

In the morning received message that health of the sister, Mrs. Ratan Prabha Jain, has worsened and the doctor is not hopeful. She had gone to

Delhi from here about 15 days ago and had to be admitted to the hospital on the second day. She remained fine for a few days but suddenly taken to the ICU only 1 day ago and then the situation worsened. I wanted to go. Talked to Neeraj who replied to go in the evening . In the afternoon, she got discharged from the hospital after her health deteriorated. Shri 108 Vibhajan Sagar ji Maharaj, who was seated in the nearby temple, was approached ,who very kindly , after preaching to her, got rid of everyone's attachment and gave "Yama Sallekhna" and gave up food etc. for 24 hours. Anjali ,who had come to Delhi only 2 days ago ,got approval from Maharaj shree for all this .

All this was shown to me through video by Chiranjeev Sangeeta. It was a very sad situation. I couldn't reach even though I wanted . Received message at 7:15 PM that sister had passed away. Chiranjeev Jinesh Kumar asked me about keeping her body till morning, I refused and was cremated in the night . The only elder left in the family was the one who passed away today. I am the only survivor of a generation. I don't know how long to live.

1 November 2021 Monday!

Left for Delhi early today after worship. The assembling was kept at Shri Ram Mandir Vivek Vihar from 10:00 to 11:00. After the ceremony,went to templeand then reached Vinita and Raju's flats. Returned at around 3:00 PM. and reached Agra at 6:30 PM., along with Neeraj, Pankaj, Sonal and Umesh .

Wednesday 8 December 2021 !

Received very sad news for the whole country today. CDS (Chief of Defense Services) Mr. Vipin Rawat along with his wife Mrs. Madhulika Rawat and 12 other army officers died in a helicopter crash near Coonoor, . One officer, who was injured and undergoing treatment, also died after 2 days. All were shocked.

The sad thing is that some people living in this country , are rejoicing over this accident under the influence of other countries/religion. It is necessary to identify and punish such people who eat the country's food. and rejoicing in the sorrows of the country.

19 January 2022 Wednesday!

Today a terrible accident happened. Mrs. Richa Jain's father, Akshay's father-in-law Mr. Chandrabhan ji Jain had died in Agra and from Delhi his two sons-in-law Mr. Ankit Jain and Mr. came to see him and were going to Firozabad with his dead body. There was a sudden accident near Tundla and elder son-in-law Mr. Ankit Jain's car collided with a parked truck and he died. Richa's younger sister was also with him who also died. Her daughter, only 18 months old, got recovered. Elder son-in-law Ankit ji's son is of 4 years. Two families have been ruined.

25.02. 2022 Friday!

Received the news of the death of Mrs. Jaimala Jain, wife of late Mrs. Abhay Kumar Jain, Mother of Mr. Rajneesh Jain in Delhi.

CHAPTER TWO

Association with State Bank of India !

Although I had been applying for jobs in various departments during my B.Sc and I had qualified State Bank of India examination in 1971 and attended interview on 13.06.1971 but could not come in the merit because by then graduation was not completed .

Even after that, I kept on preparing and applying for various jobs along with studies and as a result, at the end of 1972, I got job approvals from three departments.

These departments were Central Excise (Examination 18.07.1971 and Interview 19.07.1971), Income Tax and State Bank of India.

After severe thoughts and consultation decided to join State Bank of India and accordingly appeared for appointment in SBI ChhipitolaAgra Branch in Feb 1973.

At that time the Branch manager, who was called agent, had not less status than any government officer.There remained one Ardali ,in proper uniform ,wearing a turban ,outside the cabin of Branch Manager. He didn't allow any body to go directly to the cabin. During that time Mr. BP Sharma was the Agent/Branch Manager of Agra Main Branch and Mr. CB Dhal was the Chief Cashier.

Before the appointment, the bank issued a letter to the doctor for my medical . Dr. Vidyasagar, who lived in Ashok Nagar, to get the medical done. On getting my medical report I came back to Bank and waiting for acall , Mr.DCJain, who was the PA of the agent at that time, told that four people are underweight and they cannot be appointed at present. I was also one of these four. According to medical standards, my weight was 43 kg instead of 44. That is, 1 kg less. I found out from the conversation that one month can be given to increase the weight. Considering this as my fate I decided to go Shri Mahavirji to put an end to the resolution options.On returning from there I got a letter from the bank. According to which, after increasing the weight in a month, I had to get medical again.

So went to Dr.Vidyasagar who prescribed tablet Dianabole and instructed to eat bananas more and more and thus after a month increased the weight and got the medical done and finally on 27 March 1973, joined the cash department in the main branch of State Bank of India, Chipitola. Due to this 1 kg weight, I became one month junior to other colleagues. However, I did not have to sit at home for 1 month because I got a temporary job for this 1 month with the help of Mr. Ashok Kumar Jain and Mr. KK Sharma.

I remember another incident from that time. One day before State Bank of India's exam , I was returning from the bank on a bicycle when some children were playing gilli-danda on the way. Their gilli hit on the front wheel of my cycle. I got stuck and fell. I got hit in the head and the fellow companions took me to the doctor's place and got three or four stitches on my forehead.

From the year 1973 to 1981, I was working in the cash department in Agra main branch. I captured all the working of the cash department completely within a month or two. At that time union leader Shri Gauri Shankar Sharma, Shri B.L. Narang, Shri AK Shukla were the main ones. I didn't like the working of union leaders from the beginning and I started criticizing their workings which turned them against me . However, Shri Gauri Shankar Sharma made some favour but other people got jealous. After some time Mr. B.L. Narang and Mr. A.K. Shukla got promoted and became officers and new elections were held.

In State Bank Of India, Agra Main Branch for the Elections ,Two Groups Formed In One Group (Mr. VK Gupta group) was supported by Mr. RP Jain And The Other Group(Mr. N.K. Johar group) supported by Mr Gauri Shankar Sharma .Besides local egos , these Two groups were based on two office bearers in Delhi at the H.O. level, Mr. SN Dubbar and Mr. JN Kapoor, who were the office bearers of the same union but were staunch opponents of each other from inside. Groups were formed in the whole Delhi circle. Mr. N. K. Johar and Mr. Gauri Shankar Sharma were with Mr. S. N. Dubbar Group and V. K. Gupta and I were with J. N. Kapoor Group.

I contested for Joint Secretary with Mr. VK Gupta Group. VK Gupta stood for Secretary and Mr. OP Sharma stood for President. There were different candidates for other posts. Shri RP Jain was in the role of Bhishma Pitamah.

Our group won the election and the second group got shocked and it was reported that they were trying to create terror by bringing in the shooter and firing. Considering the fragility of the time It was decided that all the candidates should be rescued safely to their homes and this work was done. I was also dropped at around 11:30 PM . Due to being laden with garlands, everyone in the house got known that I have won.

Many things are remembered during the appointment in the main branch. , Mr.Shri Krishna Mittal, Mr. Uttam Chand Jain, Mr. SK Jain (Lalla Babu) and many others were officers/employees. All the names are not remembered now. I remember the names of many people. Mr. S. R. Nagar was the chief cashier.

There was Shri MC Jain in State Bank of India, Agra main branch, who later became a Jain monk by initiation and got samadhi .

For the construction of the house, State Bank of India Zonal Office, Agra approved the Housing Loan of Rs 40000 for construction of housevide their letter dated 25 March 1981 and received the first installment of Rs 5600, which was 80% of the cost of the land.

Cash from Agra branch went to various branches / Reserve Bank of India and a cashier was deputed with the cash, who stayed there till the entire cash got counted. For the first time I took cash on 27th November 1974 to State Bank of India ,Kasimpur(District Aligarh).

Memories of KASIMPUR !

In Kasimpur ,Head Clerk was Mr.DB Mathur of Agra, who lived in Aligarh. I moved with him to Aligarh. At that time Mr. PC Garg was the branch manager in Kasimpur.

I remember an incident from Kasimpur. One day a carpenter was working in the branch. He had a long beard growing and was a Muslim. Our colleague Mathur Sahib asked him what to put in the meat so that it melts quickly. ? His reply surprised me.He said pl ask some one who eats meat. When asked he said that he never takes NON VEG and Don't do QURBANI on EID ,the reason for this, he replied that I have read the Qur'an and there is no mention of killing innocent animals anywhere in it.

I was extremely happy to hear that there are people in other societies also who have compassion for animals/nature.

Memories of Hapur !

After this, in June 1975, I went to Hapur with cash and stayed till October

1975.

Memories of Dhampur!

I went to Dhampur in November 1975 with cash and stayed till February 1976.

19.11.1975 !

After a long time, finally it was time to leave for Dhampur. ? 100000000 packed in wooden boxes, accompanied by a police escort of 11 men and the truck proceeded towards Agra Cantt station. On reaching the station, it was found that the WAGON which had been booked, its fitment is not done yet. Fitment done and left by Bareilly passenger at 6:30 in the evening. Passenger reached Tundla Junction crossing Raja Mandi, Agra City stations. Train remained there for a long time and when started moving I opened the bed in the compartment andcontinue to reach Aligarh at 12:30. This Wagon was separated in Aligarh and was told that it will be attached to morning train. There was no idea about which train it will go. The escort officer ,contacted thSM who told that we did not know that there is a treasure in this Wagon otherwise we would not get it seperated. After 2 hours we were advised that wagon is to be attached to the other train and we lay down with our beds in the compartment next to it .In the morning Reached Chandausi at 8:00 AM.

20.11.1975 !

From Chandausi, reached Moradabad at 11:00 and met the station master, he told that wagon will be attached to the train leaving at 6:00 in the evening because the train at 11:35 is ready to leave. However on request it got attached to the train of 11:35 and reached Dhampur at 2:30PM. The head cashier and deputy head cashier were there on the station, to receive , along with Mr. SK Gupta, who was staying here before me. After opening the seal and keeping the box in the truck, reached the bank around 3:30PM. The opening of the boxes started and the work ended at 11:15 PM. I went to the head cashier's room and slept and got up at 7:00 AM when had Tea with SK Gupta & Vijay Kumar Garg .

21.11.1975 !

On reaching the bank today, I met many other employees, who were not introduced yesterday. Shri SK gupta ji had to return to Agra as he had to be relieved on my arrival. After having dinner in the evening, went to see off Gupta ji and came back to sleep.

22.11.1975 !

Arrived at the bank in the morning and finished work at 2:30 AM .Started by tempo to Sherkot to see the picture "Bandana". I liked the picture. Rabri (sweet dish) of sherkot is very famous and actually, liked a lot.

23.11.1975 !

Today was holiday and scheduled to go to Najibabad. I got up at 5:00 AM and reached the station . Janta Express departs at 5:45AM, but due to being late arrival started at 6:15AM and reached around 8:00 AM reached Najibabad. Had breakfast at the head cashier Shri Vishnoi ji and went out to see the ancient fort located there. After walking about 3 kms, what found could not be said the fort, only the gate and the boundarywere there in the name of fort. The fort is said to belong to the time of King Mordhwaj. Later it was told the place of residence of Sultana dakoo (Robber) in its forests. After returning from there, also ate food at Shri Vishnoi ji and saw the picture "Jai Santoshi Maa". Came to Dhampur and slept.

In the year 1976, on March 28, bought a cycle Hero number HU48809 whose total price was ?270 only and the stand was Rs 7.50 and the lock was Rs 4.50, the total cost was Rs 282.

Emergency Declared by Prime Minister on 25 June 1975 !

In the year 1975, emergency was imposed in the country by the then Prime Minister Smt. Indira Gandhi on June 25. And like all the departments ,in State Bank of India, the employees/officers had to maintain a daily diary in which the work details of the whole day were recorded. At the same time, overtime was almost stopped and everyone was allowed to go home only after finishing work. Special vigil was kept on the union office bearers/ employees. Emergency was lifted on 21 June 1977 after losing the election byCongress .

Memories of Banglore Jan 1979 to Feb 1979 !

Banglore Memories !

Departed for Bangalore by GT Express on 4th Jan 1979. Train was just one hour and 10 minutes late. Boarded the train at 11:45 PM. Traveled in second class due to lack of space in first class. Mr. R. D Sharma was also going to LFC. He also got in the train.

5 January 1979 !

When I opened my eyes around 6:00 AM, the train was at Bhopal. Passed time by drinking tea and having lunch. Shortly before Nagpur, an orange seller started selling oranges in the train (@?1 for 5) ,reached Nagpur after eating oranges and from there the tea-coffee cycle continued. Took the evening meal and again the tea-coffee round continued till 10:00 PM while slept.

6 January 1979 !

I did not know when it was morning. The train was running at its own high speed and at the same speed thoughts were arising in my mind about how to manage after reaching some other state, 2500 km away from Agra, where the language will also be unfamiliar. Reached Madras at about 10:00 in the morning, it was too hot . While in Agra, used to take bath with hot water every day,in Madras sat directly under the cold water tap and took a lot of bath. Here the train remained for about 3 hours. Madras - Bangalore Mail started at 0 :55 PM and landed at Bangalore City Railway Station at 8:30 PM. Mr. SK Mittal was present along with another person. I was introduced to the person who hails from Agra and doing business in bangalore .

7 January 1979 !

Living in Bangalore is too much of a hassle. Despite a lot of running around, still haven't been able to get a room. Today, I met the Deputy General Secretary in Bangalore State Bank. Arranged a stay at the holiday home with his help. A coconut seller ,outside the holiday home ,a little boy used to sit there and whenever I used to go to RBI, my two daughters, Neeru and Neetu, who were around 6 years and 4 years old at that time, used to come down and hide themselves against stairs ,on my arrival they appered ang got Coconut. This was their daily routine till we remain in Banglore.

Some memories from during my stay in Bangalore!

There are many places to visit in Bangalore, some of which are:

Ulsoor Lake: Ideal place for Boating

Cabbage Park: Perfect place for kids, small train and lots of toys

Museum: Very useful for science students Timings: 10:00 AM to 5:00 PM

Lal Bagh Garden: Variety of flowering plants and small aquarium

Assembly (deal): There is special lighting on Sundays

MG Road Shopping Center : For the wealthy. There is a government organization called Kaveri which has most of the sandalwood items and many other items available at reasonable rates.

Jain Mandir: Digambar Jain Temple Chickpet, New Road Near Abhinay Theatre, Shwetambar Jain Temple, Chickpet

Note boxes were opened in Reserve Bank of India, Bangalore from 22 January 1979 to 22 February 1979 and 15000 bundles of one denomination of 15000000 notes were kept in different wins.

There are many places to visit in Mysore:

1.Vrindaban Gardens --- Daily Lighting from 6.30 PM to 7.30 PM ticket Rs25/-,Boating @30 p

2.Srirangapatnam Temple-- Situated on the way from Bangalore to Mysore. Tickets for ?25 per person.

3. Zoo - Entrance ?1

4. Maharaja's Palace ----Entrance ?1

5. Art Gallery --- Entrance ?1

6.Two Jain Temples

Shravanabelagola (Gomateshwara) --- 4 hours from Bangalore, Muni Vidyanand Nilaya (Dharamsala) in Shravanabelagola has rooms (attach bath and kitchen) for ? 5 and beds for ? 1. There are also other dharamshalas and guest houses. I

1 Timings are from 6:30 AM to 6:30 PM.

2. Chandra Giri, this is the second mountain. There are 13 temples and a cave of Bhadrabahu Swami (who was the last Shrut Kevali) where his feet are established. Apart from this, Bhandar Basadi, Akkan Basti and Jinnathpur temples are also worth seeing.

In Madras :

Digambar Jain Temple, Sokarpet, Subrahmanyam Street, Madras and Second Chandanapam Street No. One (Near Madras Central Railway Station) I Shvetambara Temple - Marwari Temple Manabalam, GN Chetty Road Madras-17 I About 15 temples Jain temples in Madras are reported.

Memories of Nagpur!

In May 1979, I went to Nagpur with the treasury, to get the notes counted in the Reserve Bank of India.

Stayed at Shri Gurudev Lodge, Modi No. 3, Sitabardi in Nagpur.

Jain Temple and Dharamshala are in Itwari, which is about 5 kms from the station.

Main Market - Itwari, Sitabardi, Sadar, Mahal.

Place to visit - Ambazari, Seminar HillsRamtek Digambar Jain Atishaya Kshetra is located about 40 kms away and train and bus facility is available from Nagpur to reach here.

Jain Temples - There are 8 Vedies of Lord Shri Shantinath and other Gods. Dharamsala is nearby. The temple is worth visiting.

Ram Mandir - Ram temple is situated by climbing about 450 steps. It is said that Shri Ram ji came here during the exile of 14 years.

People from far and wide had come during my stay in Nagpur. In meeting with them, I got various information about the customs, living habits of different places.

The cashier who came from Kohima (Nagaland) told that Kohima is a very cold area. Due to the severe heat of Nagpur, he was finding it very difficult to stay here. Describing the strange things of the Nagas in Kohima, he said that the behavior of the Nagas, although not very unusual, turns violent when people drink Madu (liquor). Not obeying is a disaster. Others hate stealing and lying. They treat women with great respect.

An incident about this is such that a resident of Kerala got transferred to the State Bank of India, Kohima branch. One of his chickens was killed and eaten by a Naga (Due to the abundance of chickens, Nagas do not consider it theft). When he came to know about this, he got angry and called that Naga a thief. Just on this matter many Nagas reached his house together in the night to kill him. But his wife opened the door and stood in the middle of the door. When the Naga asked her to leave, he said that only after killing me, you could go inside. Due to respect for the woman, at that time they left saying that how long will you save him, will see tomorrow. To find out the seriousness of the situation the person was transferred out of Kohima and went under the supervision of the police, otherwise what would have happened to him.

There are fights in the picture halls due to the disobedience of the Nagas who drink the Madu. The Nagas after drinking the Madu go to the picture and two persons sit on the same seat. At the slightest protest by the person nearby, the fight starts.

In Kohima, the old man is called Kokai and is given full respect. To settle any kind of dispute, the Kokai of the village gather together and decide and their decision is valid.

There, love is not considered a sin. Boys and girls go to a party during the night, then the girl tells her parents where I am going and when I will return. Often the girl's mother herself sends her by feeding her contraceptive pill. and she is free to stay out all night.

According to the representative from Shillong, the girl can be ordered among other things by staying in a hotel in Shillong and reaches the room. There, no one bothers the police etc.

In the year 1982 (15.10.1982) for the first time old Lambretta scooter WBN2091 was purchased from Mr.BK Batham, who was working in the bank, for ?3000. Bought scooter UPU7157 on 04.03.1984, bought scooter VIJAY SUPER CPB3338 on 11.05.1987.

Memories of Pilua ! 18.08.1981 - 19.11.1983 !

After the promotion as Cash Officer in December 1980, posted as Cash Officer in Pilua (District Etah) from 1981 to 1983. Many incidents there are in mind.

Pilua is located at a distance of about 10 kms from Etah (on Etah-Aligarh road). I lived with family in Etah in the house of Mr. Saxena sahib on Thandi Sarak in two room set.

At that time Mr. Khanna ji was the branch manager in Pilua. He used to go by scooter from Etah. I used to accompany him. On the 4th mile on the way, there was Sardar ji's hotel. We used to stay there. Khanna ji opened their two accounts at Pilua branch. He used to give some amount every day for deposit in those accounts. On returning in the evening, pass books handed over to him . Sometimes we used to eat cold kheer at that hotel there.

Once on returning from Pilua, the scooter was not fitted with Stepney. I was trying to sit with the help of Stepney as usual and got unbalanced and fell badly. Everyone around panicked. Immediately picked me up but I didn't hurt much. People told that the way I had fallen, anything could have happened.

Buses and aces ply from Pilua to Etah. An ace wala, who was also a bank loanee, came to know that he was formerly a dacoit and now drives an ace after surrender. He had a black horse in his ace and once he The horseshoe was given to me at no cost. When the inspection took place in Pilua, the inspector also had to stay in Etah. His name is not remembered but he was a good person and was also associated with a film organization from Mumbai. He was vegetarian. He did not like hotel food and used to eat food at home with me. He also used to admire Sushma's food.

Once we got late while leaving the bank from Pilua and one bus left and we kept waiting for the second bus. The first bus met with an accident before Etah and this information was with the landlord but he did not tell Sushma(my wife). When I reached home, he became happy and said we were worried but did not inform your family otherwise she would be worried .

In front of the bank in Pilua there was the clinic of Dr. S. D. Sharma who was BAMS .His investigation was amazing. I used to complain of itching in my eyes often due to cold, for which he prescribed Pyrimon medicine which was suitable . We ,alongwith veterinary doctor Saxena sahib used to take lunch together. On one Saturday, Mr. RS Verma, agricultural assistant and Ashok, clerk, said to finish before 2.00 PM, and see the picture from

3:00 PM at Etah.After completing the work in a hurry, everyone left for Etah at about 1.35 PM. Incidentally ,around 2:00 PM the Assistant General Manager reached Pilua from Agra and seen the bank closed.He asked a walking person about when the bank was closed. The person looked around and said probably not opened today. This must have surprised the Assistant general manager.

Dr S D Sharma came up and told the AGM fact about a bit early closing.However ,AGM got furious and explanations of all were called and we had to cut Sorry figure for early closure of the Branch.
Plantation with the village head on the occasion of Bank Day July 1at Pilua !

During my appointment in Pilua,The Chief Cashier in SBI Etah was Mr. S.C. Gupta,friendship with him is continued .He is residing at Dayal Bagh Agra .His wife passed away in April 2021.
On 5th May 1983 I went to Dehradun for 15 days training.

Memories of Nagar Mahapalika Agra Branch ! 21.11.1983 - 19.06.1985
In the year 1983, I got transferred from Pilua to Agra and was posted as Cash Officer in Nagar Mahapalika Agra Branch. Mr. HM Bhatnagar was the Branch Manager and Mr. MM Puri was the Accountant, who was from Delhi. Old acquaintances were in the staff, some of whom remember the names of Som Prakash Garg who was working as Teller and very jolly in nature, Mr. Rajeev Sharma who was the son of my former teacher Shri Chandra Pal Ji Sharma.
At that time Mr. VK Pushp was the Regional Manager who was very strict administrator.

Memories of Shikohabad Branch! 18.10.1985 - 16.06.187 - 11.07.1991
In the year 1987 I was transferred from Agra to Shikohabad main branch. At that time Mr. K. R.K. Sinha was the Branch Manager, Shri RkGupta was field officer (who later got murdered in Bhogaon Brach alongwith one other officer), Shri G C Chahar was accountant who was of jolly nature. Later on, Mr. GC Tandon,of Mathura posted as Branch Manager with whom my tuning was not good. He tried to defame me and started imposing more and more work on my seat, continuously giving false feedback to regional office against me .When the file of correspondance got big and I sent his complaint to Mr. Umaid Singh, General Secretary SBI Officers' Association and alonwith I sent a direct letter against him to the General Manager, which was wrong as per service rules, but the General Manager decided on

it in my favour.

Mr. SK Bhatura was the Regional Manager at that time. Once came to the branch and said that what did you write to Umaid Singh that he called me at 12:00 AM, in the night and asked to solve your problem. I did not say anything. Bhatura Sahib understood my problems and transferred from Main Branch to ADB (Agriculture Development Branch), Shikohabad, where Mr. BP Amoria was the Branch Manager, who was the Staff Cell Incharge (Region 2) at the time of my posting in Pilua. I had fine tuning with him.

In May 1989, the Jawahar Small Industries Exhibition was held at Ramlila Ground in Shikohabad. The stall of State Bank of India ADB Shikohabad was inaugurated by the District Magistrate Firozabad on 18 May 1989.

Later Mr. Subhash Sharma got posted as Branch Manager and my promotion (MM-II) could be due to these two branch managers Mr BPAmoria and Mr. Subhash Sharma otherwise Mr. GC Tandon had spoiled my report badly.

Bought a new Bajaj Cub scooter on 7.06.1989 for ?12305/26 while staying in Shikohabad and bought a red color Maruti 800 car (1985 model) on 27.09.1990 for ?80000 from Mr. Kapurchand Maheshwari, Agra.

Memories of Agra Branch! 16.07.1991 - 04.06.1994

In Agra branch, I was asked to work of current account incharge, where many shortcomings, some of which were very serious in nature,were highlighed to the Assistant General Manager. Though he wrote "Appreciate" on the note sent by me, but there was a glimpse of change in his behavior to me. Later ,after a couple of times he said that it is not proper to give everything in writing.

Later I got posted at COD Extension Counter, Kendriya Vidyalaya Extension Counter, 509 Extension Counter and finally at Hotel Mughal Extension Counter, where I had to directly talk to the Deputy General Manager for serious lapses.

The Manager of Hotel Mughal used to deal in share market and third party checks of large amounts were purchased(DDpurchase) and deposited in his account on the same dayand he used to withdraw the money immediately. This practice was going on for many years. As such purchasing of cheques was not in my jurisdiction, I declined. He called the DGM directly. from DGM's office, an assistant asked me to get his work done .I politely refused and when he pressurised , I asked to provide orders in writing. No such orders ever got and this wrong practice remained closed till my posting ther at .

On 4th June 1994, I was relieved from Agra branch to report to the Zonal Office (Region One).

Memories of Seo Ka Bazar ,Agra Branch! 11.06.1994 - 08.05.1997

On 7th June 1994, I was interviewed by the Assistant General Manager (Region One) Mr. A S Sharma about further posting. He told me about the image of Seo Ka Bazar branch, Agra and asked if I could work hard for its smooth running. I confirmed and On 11th June 1994 I was placed with orders for Branch Manager Seo Ka Bazar Branch, Agra.

From 1994 to 1997, I remained ,as Branch Manager, in State Bank of India's Seo Ka Bazar, Agra branch as Branch Manager.

It was a pleasure to get the post of branch manager of a big branch for the first time, but the image of the branch was very bad. It was not easy to do all the hard work and planning to run the branch smoothly. There had been some persons in past whose activities and character have tarnished the image of the branch.

I took over from Mr. SC Gupta.The award staff included Shri GP Gupta, Shri RC Sharma (Tellor), Shri LP Sharma, Shri Gopal Babu, Shri AK Jain, Shri KC Gupta, Shri Ramchandra, Shri Yogendra Kumar, Shri KR Madhukar, Shri MN Sharma. , Mr. Basant Singh, Mr. Ashok Kohli, Mr. Tarun, Mr. Umesh Kumar, Mr. L. N. Rohatgi, Y. K. Dixit, D. C. Garg. The subordinate staff consists of Mr. Jesus, Foran Singh, Ram Singh, Ramsevak, Ramesh Chand Solanki and Security guards were Mr. Santoshi Lal, Mr. Khyaliram, Mr. Ramesh Singh, Mr. Lekhraj Singh.

The condition of Seo Ka Bazar, Agra Branch was really pathetic. The employees in the cash department were having fun. The cash had accumulated so much that there was no space left in the strong room. The parties coming to get the draft were got returned for want of space to keep the cash and the party once left did not come again to the bank. This was the result of not taking proper action in this regard by the former branch managers. I reviewed the situation and after deliberations came to the conclusion that to divert cash,I had to find branches where payments are high and cash deposits are low. Found two such branches, SIB, Agra and Nunhai, Agra. I started sending cash in coordination with them. Cash department was instructed that no draft would be returned without my permission.

After reviewing again after 1 week, it was found that no party to make big drafts came. I alongwith F.o. Mr Lachwani visited a number of High value drafts purchasers.One of such client told the old story of the Branch.According to him no body in the Brach ever bothered to resolve their problem and avoided to talk. There had been stink of liquor in the premises after 2.00 PM.He advised me that I am small in stature, get yourself saved from such people. Such thougts among public were tarnishing the image of the branch, as well as of State Bank of India. It was getting worse. Well, somehow the traders were requested to visit once and see if there is any problem still persist. In this way the draft business got increasing and it was so much that the major income of the Branch was from draft business .However,Cash keeping situation was still critical, so contacted Karhal branch where Mr. SK Gupta was the branch manager and started sending huge amount of cash there and gradually there was enough space in the strong room to keep the incoming cash.

There was an employee who was rarely seen in the branch. When I saw his holiday record, the debit balance of 6 months was running, and no branch manager has taken any action against him till now. He is getting salary of every month regularly. I ordered to pay salary only for the number of days hejoined the bank in a month. He attended for 14 days on that month and I instructed to pay his salary for 14 days.Being annoyed with it he rushed to my room and asked why his salary had cut. When I asked him how many days he had in the Branch, then he remained silent and said what will I feed my children? I said that he should have thought it before being absent. I warned him that from next month 15 days salary will be deducted so that your six months leave can be adjusted. He got a little agitated and then left. I came to know more about him that he had started some shoe business. got fond of lottery and his condition became very pathetic. On my persuasion he promised me that he would not play lottery anymore and will also come to bank regularly .This was what I wanted. I aroused interest in him and kept doing that work. But I did not know that he was planning to cheat the bank along with work. Later it was discovered that he had embezzled money by transferring two and a half lakh rupees from an account to his wife's account and left the bank as well as the city (Agra). He had two small children. When he couldn't traced for a long time it was feared that he might have taken a step like suicide I got distracted by this apprehension. I thought, what was the fault of the small children in this? In this case the bank set up the inquiry and also found twwithdrawal forms of my tenure in which he had withdrawn 10000 and 5000 from the inoperative accounts at his witness. This payment was done by the teller on his responsibility . In this case I was also given a charge sheet for "Vicarious Responsibility" as Branch Manager. After many years it was found that he was doing business in Bangalore and moved the family to Bangalore. Later he was seen in Agra running a hotel.

Customer Relations Program was organized at the branch on 21st December 1994.

There was an incident of 1996. Assistant General Manager Mr. Manohar Lal ji told me to post Mr. Mathur ji (officer) to my branch and asked to keep him by giving him light work. On asking it was revealed that Mr. Mathur ji was a case of Psychological Disorder. He used to leave home for the bank and got back without entering the bank. It is possible that there was a phobia, which happened in some other branch due to some mistake or other reason.

I gave approval and the next day Mathur ji was brought to the bank by his wife. Mathur sahib seemed perfectly fine in the conversation. His style of working was appreciated from the old branches. He was not given any work and asked to talk to the staff. In the evening his wife came to pick him up and he went back home. The program continued. He was given assignments as per his interest.

After a few days his wife came and said that Mathur Sahab is not ready to come. I went to his house and explained to Mathur Sahib, then he started coming again to the bank.

One day his wife came and told in a very sad state that the children are growing up, their fees are not being arranged because Mathur Sahab's salary has not been received for many months. Although Mathur Sahab's elder brother had a good business but today No one in the world wants to help anyone except some exceptionals. His wife was running the house by sewing clothes.

This situation was very pathetic and painful but I was also not able to do anything. I told them to just bring them to the bank . This happened for few days but in the end he stopped coming completely.

This incident gave an impression that luck factor in once life had a very strong role. Despite Mathur's good job, wife and children were living in deprivation. Later it was found that Mathur Sahib had taken voluntary retirement and the service period was less than 20 years, he did not even get the facility of pension. It is also known that later he was cured and started cooperating in business with his elder brother. All this proves the concept of Karma Siddhanta is very much true.

On Thursday, 8th May 1997, I was relieved to work as Manager Agriculture in Aligarh City branch from Seo ka Bazar, Agra.

Memories of Aligarh City Branch ! 24.05.1997 - 7.11.1998

I was deputed to Aligarh City branch on Thursday, 8th May 1997, as Manager Agriculture. It was a Scale 3 post and I was informed that this posting was given because of your performance in Seo ka Bazar, Agra.. I was not interested and tried my best by continuous visits to Head Office Delhi to change the post from 9th May 1997 to 23rd May 1997 (15 days) but got no success and finally I had to join Aligarh City branch.

I joined Aligarh City Branch on 24 May 1997 ,Saturday. The Chief Manager was Mr. YRS Chauhan. Prior to me, the Manager Agriculture was Mr. DS Bisht, whom I relieved for Meerut on June 5, 1997.

I had three field officers Mr. Mahesh Chand Jain who was from Mathura, Mr. Nayan Singh who was from Delhi and Mr. DS Tayal who was from Ghaziabad. Later Mr. S. C. Maggo, who was from Delhi, was also with me as field officers. There was another field officer, whose name I can not remember, who used to tell by some calculation whether there is a male/female child in the womb.

In Aligarh, I rented a room at Kapoori Bhawan (which was near a Jain temple) in Lekhraj Nagar.

On 28 June 1997, I accompanied Inspector Mr. SV Mani to Agra to drop him for Bhopal. He had ticket for train from Agra to Bhopal. I remember the incident at that time.

There became a programme to have lunch at home at Agra with the Inspector sir. Wife Sushma Jain Told this over the phone. And she had prepared lunch. When we had lunch, there was no onion and garlic because we don't use them. I thought he might not like to eat without onion and garlic. He not only ate it fiercely but also said that this is the first time I had taken such delicious food without onion and garlic. I joked that the smell of onion and garlic removes the shortcomings of bad food, so he started laughing.

There was a lot of work in the Agriculture Division in Aligarh City as well as various court cases were pending . Some times one had to go to Allahabad High Court also. To give counter affidavit in a case I went to

Allahabad on 01.08.1997, to contact Arun Kumar Mishra Advocate High Court. Started from Aligarh by Sangam Express on 30.07.1997, discussed with lawyer on 31.07.1997 and remained in the High Court for the whole day on 01.08.1997 ,returned back by Prayagraj in the evening and reached Aligarh at 4:30 AM on 2nd August .

Took joining time from 7th August 1997 to 13th August 1997 and went to visit Shri Sammed Shikharji on 7th August.

Aligarh City branch had an account of CDF (Central Dairy Form), which had become cronic NPA. Central Dairy Farm was a Uttar Pradesh government undertaking run by government officials. Recovery in the account could not be made from the government. On 3rd September 1997 I went to CDF factory to meet the MD and General Manager.

On October 22, 1997, when I again visited the CDF, two officers were not present there. Only the Dairy Incharge was available. Though the unit named a dairy farm, but meat was also processed there. He told that before slaughtering an animal, it got shot with a bullet in forehead that made it unconscious.

Seeing the procedure here, it was realized that running a business should not the job of the government . Bank had to settle this account with the help from Chief Minister's Office through the General Manager New Delhi for a very small amount and got closed.

The mission of fully computerisation of Aligarh City branch started in December 1997. I could not avail my leave of 26 December,27 December ,sanctioned earlier. On 29 December 1997, Aligarh City branch got fully computerized.

On 18 January 1998, Pulse Polio Program was organized in 2 villages, Ilyaspur and Mehrabad.

8 February 1998 Sunday!

Today I have been deputed to go to Hyderabad training and reached Delhi and stayed with Raju (RajeshkumarJain).

9 February 1998 Monday!

Woke up today at 3:30. Raju had booked for a taxi at night. The taxi arrived at 4:00 AM. Reported after reaching the airport at around 5:00 PM and kept moving around the airport after completing the check-in formalities. Indian Airlines flight no. 940 was scheduled at 6:20. Board on Airbus 320 at 6.10 AM. Theaeroplane took off at about 6:30 and arrived at 8:20 at Hyderabad. There was no water at the airport. The matter was being reported by the staff. Left for SBIRD (near Lingampalli) by prepaid taxi. Reported at the center around 9:30 AM and stayed in room no. 308 with Mr. B. Satyanarayana from SBI ADB Visakhapatnam. In the evening, accompanied by Mr. A. Sarkar and Tapas Banerjee went to see the Charminar. Bus no. 216 / 217 goes to Mehndi Patnam and from there bus no. 65 / 66 reaches Charminar.

Returning from there had fruit and milk and slept .

10 February 1998 Tuesday!

Woke up today at 7:00 AM. ,had a cup of tea in the room, chanted some poojan/ bhajans. Today was Chaturdashi. I wanted to go to the temple but could not. Arrived at the lecture room. In the evening, saw the "Sound and Light" program at the Golconda Fort. The program was in Hindi and I liked it. Seeing the ruins of the fort built in the year 1347, it gives the impression that everything is perishable. Between 13th century to the sixteenth century How many ups and downs were there, in the life of various kings associated with this fort .

Made called to Agra/Delhi at night .

11 February 1998 Wednesday!

Worshiped at the room itself this morning.I was restless because I didn't go to the temple for 3 days. After breakfast, Mr. Ahmed told many things about Israel in the lecture room. Fruit juice is cheaper there than water . Other items are much more expensive than in Mumbai. In the evening a cultural program was organized by CARE attended . Mrs. and Mr. RK Sinha (Principal SBI RD) was also present.

12 February 1998 Thursday!

Today there was a program to visit APAD and Walamtri. After breakfast at 9:00 AM, started by Agro's VAN. Reached APAD in about 30 minutes where R. Subramaniam Ready, Agriculture Engineer provided information about various agricultural implements. From there Reached Walamtri in about 15 minutes, where information about various schemes as well as information about Sprinkle and Dip Irrigation was given in the form of practical. Arrived at Birla Mandir. The temple is very beautiful and is on a hill near Hussain Sagar Lake. Hyderabad and Secunderabad are visible from inside the temple. After returning, buy some pearl jewelery from Mangat Rai Jewelers, Basir Bagh and reached Charminar from where Rickshaw arranged for the Jain temple Begum Bazar . There are many idols in the temple.

13 February 1998 Friday !

Today in the evening went to Mehandipatnam. From there on my way to

Charminar by Bus No. 66G, a "Mahavir Hospital", which is near the wooden bridge and a short distance from Mehndipatnam, appeared. Immediately taken off the bus because it was of the other route. From there ,by tempo, went to "Agapura Jain Temple". There are many idols. Idols of Lord Chandraprabhu, Lord Parasnath and Lord Mahavira are very attractive. I went to the temple of Caravan from Agapura but could not reach the temple even after a lot of trouble but reached the Jain Shwetambar temple in Dadabari and had darshan there. Came back at 8:45 PM.

14 February 1998 Saturday!

Reached Chadarghat Jain Temple at 1:00 PM today via Mehndipatnam. Temple is in good shape. After visiting the temple, visited the museum and then came SBIRD from Bashir Bagh to Mangat Rai for some shopping. At 5:35 AM arrived at the airport by auto rickshaw due to non-availability of taxi. Checking was being announced on arrival. The plane took off at 7:30 PM and was flying at a speed of 850 kmph at an altitude of 28000 feet, leaving Nagpur, Gwalior Agra, reached Delhi at 9:25. On enquiring for the taxi, it was found that they are asking for excess fare. So, got prepaid taxi and at around 11:30 AM reached Raju's flat D30, Jhilmil Colony, Delhi .

15 February 1998 Sunday!

This morning there was a programme to go to Tijara ji with Vinita , Jinesh Kumar, Bobby etc. On reaching Tijara ji at around 8:45, it was found that the main bedi's prakshaal is done at 6:45 and at others ,can be done till 10:00. Immediately after taking a bath arrived for Abhishek. Had blessings to see God. Later Chiranjeev Neeru and Ankit had come with Shri Suresh Chand ji. At "Kasan" saw the idols found from the ground, which are Lord Parasnath as well as many other Gods. After returning from Shalimar Bagh at 7:30 PM, reached Jhilmil Colony at Raju's flat.

16 February 1998 Monday!

Arrived at Nizamuddin railway station today at 6:45 AM by taxi and reached Raja Mandi, Agra at 9:30 AM by Taj. Today due to elections, no one was found and could reach home after calling Neeraj by phone.

30 June 1998 Tuesday!

Today, as per the order of the Assistant General Manager, went to Agra to collect sticks and monuments to be given to old people on 1st July 1998, as Bank Day celebratios, along with tree plantation, a program was also organized by AMU branch at Tehsil .

On 7th November 1998, I was relieved from Aligarh City branch to take over as Branch Manager in Avagarh branch.

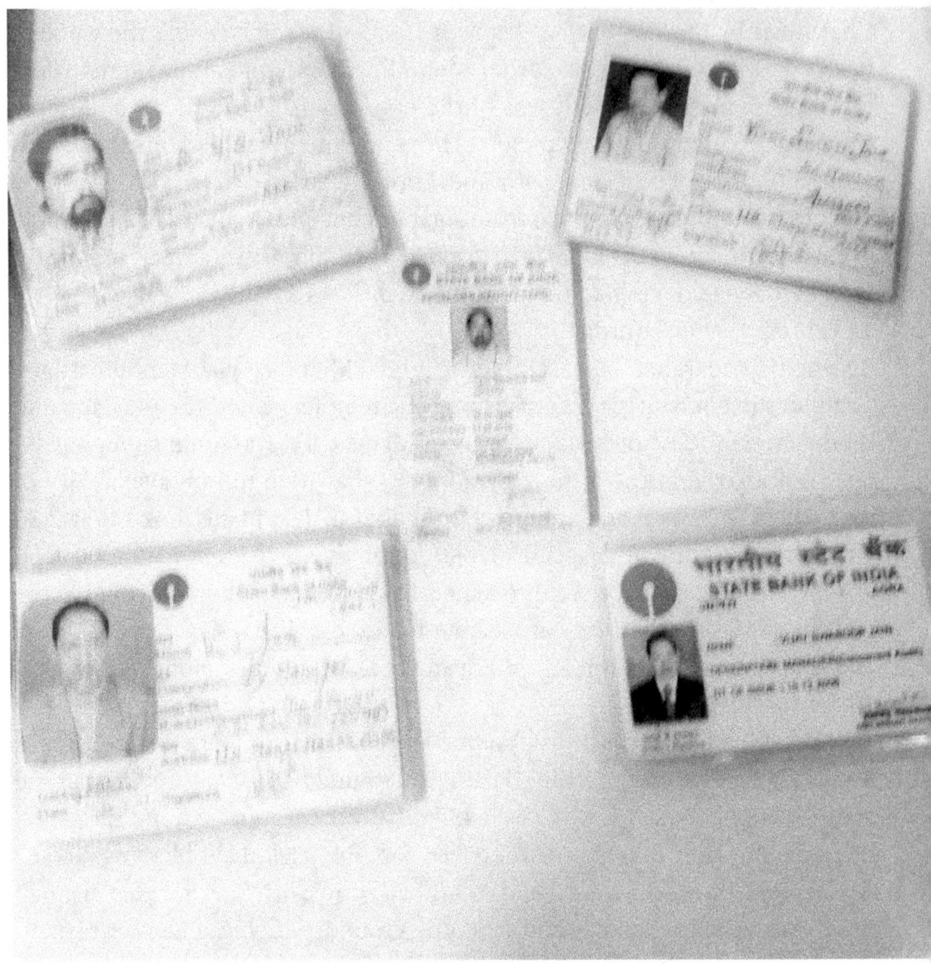

Identity Cards issued By Bank in various Branches !

Memories of Awagarh Branch ! 09.11.1998 -

November 8, 1998 ,Today went to Shri Mahavirji and came back in the evening.

9 Nov 1998 -Joined as Branch Manager, Awagarh Branch. The branch is located in Mr. Prem Kishore ji's building, going down a small street in the main market. The maintenance and cleanliness of the branch is not good.

November 14, 1998 -Children's day program was organized in Padam Shri Jain Vidyalaya Awagarh today.

16 November 1998 -Full fledged working as Branch manager, State Bank of India Awagarh started .

19 November 1998 -Reached zonal office to discuss some issues where

it was told that on November 23, the Deputy General Manager can visit the branch. Only 2 days were in between and the condition of the branch was not good. I decided to get painting and cleaning. When I returned home from zonal office in the evening, dehydration happened and I had to be admitted to Dr. BK Gupta's nursing home. Now there is a lot of problem. I called Field Officer JT Singh Ji and acountant Shri RK Jhingran and instructed them to get whitewashed and cleaning from tomorrow morning and get the same completed withen two days . I also reached the branch on 21st in the condition of illness.

November 23, 1998 - Awagarh branch was visited by Assistant General Manager Mr. PK Kulshrestha along with Deputy General Manager Mr. Rajkumar ji .

November 27, 1998 - today called a meeting of the entire staff of the branch and discussed various problems.

January 1, 2000 - Today, a dental check up camp and welcome of the families of the Kargil martyrs.

were organized by the bank !

welcome of the families of the Kargil martyrs!

14 March 2000 -Veterinary camp was organized in village Mishakhurd.

Vaternity Camp organised !

I was interviewed for MM-III (from 1.11.1998) on 21st June 2000 at Zonal Office Agra and from there I was given a relieving letter for Zonal Office Jaipur. Next day on 22nd June 2000 I handed over the charge of Awagarh branch to Mr. J.T Singh and I got relieved .

Memories of Jhujhunu Branch !

Departed for Jaipur on Friday 23 June 2000 and reported to Zonal Office Jaipur on Saturday 24 June 2000 where I was allotted Region 4. Assistant General Manager Mr. KK Kashyap, Chief Manager Mr. Madan Jeet Singh, Mr. Kamal Dutt Sharma (Staff cell Incharge), Zonal Secretary Mr. PN Sharma, Zonal President Mr. Dhir, Mr. Ghanshyam Sharma, Treasury besides other officers the names of whom are not remember.

On 28 June 2000 - I received the letter of appointment to the post of Accountant in Jhunjhunu and on 29 June I reported in Jhunjhunu.

30 June - took some charge on 1 July and left for Agra on 1 July. From 3 July to 17 July Took HTC (Home Travel Concession).

In connection with the inquiry of Seo ka Bazar Agra Branch, reached at

Delhi Head Office on 5th July and 6th July, met Mr. T N Goyal and Mr. B. K. Bhog Inquiry Officer. I took charge from 24th to 26th July but due to ill health left for Agra on 26th July. I reached Agra on 27th July and had to be admitted to the hospital.

On 18 September 2000 I left Agra for Jaipur and met the AGM. After categorically refused to change posting, I reached Jhunjhunu and took charge on 19.09.2000 from Mr. Banwari Lal, who was the Acting Accountant.

On November 28, 2000, I shifted to house no. C-90, Rico Colony in Jhunjhunu. Due to the onset of winter season, I got quilt and mattresses.

There was also a Jain temple (small chaityalaya) in RIICO Colony where Abhishek-Puja was performed. On 24 September 2000, a program was held at H-39 Rico Industrial Area at Shri Shikhar Chand Jain, in which many Jain families participated.

Branch Manager in Jhunjhunu was Mr. G C Goel, Mr. M. P. Jain was the field officer. There is an incident that around 7:00 in the evening we were in the bank and Mr. M. P. Jain's motorcycle was parked outside. A couple in the car with their children came along and put the car in neutral, the husband got down from the car and the child put the gear on. The car climbed on Jain Sahab's motorcycle and the motorcycle got a lot of dent. Immediately took the motorcycle to the agency for assessment of damage . The agency owner shared his experience with State Bank. He told that he started this work 10-12 years ago in PMRY by taking loan from State Bank of India and is the owner of the agency today. Glad to hear that.

On 18 May 2001, I was given a farewell party in Jhunjhunu branch and on 19 May 2001, I was relieved from Jhunjhunu for Deeg branch. After attending the seminar on 20th June, I went to visit Shri Mahavir ji on 21st May and joined Deeg branch on 23rd May 2001.

Memories of Deeg Branch !

I joined Deeg Branch as Branch Manager on 23rd May 2001. Field Officer Shri UC Bansal,
, Accountant Mr., other staff were Mr. Moolchand, Mr. TD Gupta, Mr. Hoti Lal, Mr. Fazru Khan, Mr. Radha Raman Sharma.

By the time I reached the branch, there was a crowd of farmers in the branch because the former branch manager had already been relieved, so the new loans and renewals of the farmers were on hold. Instructions were given to start sanctioning . Gradually, all the people in the branch got familiar and the work of the bank started running smoothly.

Shri Fazru Khan was a poet and he told that he had written "Khandakavya" on 20 out of 24 Jain Tirthankaras.

From 6.6.2001 to 9.6.2001, I was deputed to Ajmer Training Center for training on "NPA Management". I reached Ajmer on 6th at 7:30 AM. There Mr. DC Gangwal Assistant General Manager (Training) and other faculty members Shri Hanuman Prasad, Shri Suresh Besh, Shri SD Sharma The training was very beneficial and I also visited many places of Ajmer. First in the evening I went to the Dargah of Khwaja Chishti and saw the two and a half day hut which was built by Qutubuddin Aibak in 1200 AD. There are ruins of Jain/Hindu temples. The fact is that there had been a Jain Sanskrit school at this place, which was demolished and got converted within two and a half days. This is an example of the bigotry and barbarism of the Mughal Empire. Surely the dargah must have been built in the same way by destroying the temples.

In the dargah, one of the two big pots can cook 60 Quintal of rice and the other 120 Quintals of rice. On returning see the temple of Bajranggarh, which is at a great height, and before that the 'Anand Sagar Lake' which is very huge .

07.06.2001 -Waking up in the morning after taking bath, went to Soni ji's nasia. On the main Vedi there is a huge Lord 1008 Shri Aadinath and some other Gods. Many other Gods are also seated on the second and third bed.

Departed by bus at 7:30 AM for Nareli which is about 15 kms from Ajmer. There the grand construction of Gyanodaya Teerth is going on with the blessings of Shri 108 Shri Sudhasagar Ji Maharaj. Dharamshala, Bhojanalaya, Gaushala in a vast area of 297 Bigha .Apart from the rabbit park, there are plans for huge construction on the mountain. At present, 365 stairs and three temples have been built for the mountain. In the first temple, the first Tirthankar of the past, the first Tirthankar of the present and the first Tirthankar of the future are seated. Lord Shantinath, Kunthnath, Arnath and in the third temple Lord Adinath, Sheetal Nath, Mahavir are seated. As told by one Aryaka Mata ji gods usually come in the night to worship /pray many people have heard their conversations.

8 June 2001

This morning, in the temple of Chhoti Nasiya ji, Moolnayak Bhagwan 1008 Adinath ji is enthroned in black stone. Other altars God are seated. Departed for Pushkar ji around 4:00 in the evening, after passing through various hill roads, reached Pushkar ji within about 20-25 minutes. Baths were going on at various ghats. The water is not clean. Some are filled with water from tube wells. The main temple is of Shri Brahma ji, which is quite huge. There are also two Jain temples. Could have darshan in which 1008 Lord Mahavir is seated in huge form and some other Gods also. I could not visit the second temple and returned back to Ajmer at 8:00 PM.

09.06. 2001

After closing the session today, at around 1:00 PM. I left for Delhi by Shatabdi Express at 3:30 PM.

There was a Single Officer Branch "Thoon" under the control of Deeg branch, for which I had to go for monthly inspection. On 30th May I reached for first such monthly inspection.

On June 21, 2001, a farmers seminar and veterinary camp was organized in village Sheeshbara, in which Dr. BD Sharma, Veterinary Officer himself appeared. Agreements were made at the site itself. Medicines and medicines were distributed to about 300 animals.

Inspection of Deeg branch was completed on 1st January 2002 by Mr. A C Tandon (Manager Inspection). On 2nd January morning I went to Bharatpur with Mr. Tandon.

9 March 2002 got fixed for complete computerization of Deeg branch . The branch was fully computerized and work started from 11th March 2002. The profit of the branch as on 31st March 2002 was 1.36 crores.

Beekeeping loans were also disbursed in Deeg branch along with other loans. I went to Narholi village on 3 February 2003 for one such post-loan survey and got a lot of information about beekeeping. Bees are kept in separate boxes which are their homes, and such a small organism is so sensitive that a fly from another box cannot enter their house. If a bee from another box would come near the other box ,house owner bees of that box got it drive away. The queen bee lays the eggs and the rest protect them. In the morning they are released into the flower fields, from where they collect pollen and make honey in their boxes. All the bees return to their homes. The method of extracting honey is scientific. The flies are removed and hung in the drum and the honey droplets drip from the strong wind and collect in the drum and the bees are not harmed.

However, honey is not edible because it is a vomit of Bees and microorganisms are always there and as such it is not vegetarian.

On 15 11 2002, I was called to give a lecture regarding bank services in

Government Girls' Secondary School, Deeg.

The profit of Deeg branch as on 31st March 2003 was 1.53 crores.

I was given farewell at Deeg branch on Friday 9th May 2003 and relieved on Saturday 10th May 2003 to take over the charge of Branch Manager, State Bank of India Tajganj Agra. I went to Delhi on 12th May 2003 and went to Shri Mahavirji on Tuesday, 13th May 2003. . Returned from Shri Mahavirji, reported at Tajganj branch on Wednesday, May 14, 2003.

Memories of Tajganj Branch !

On 14 May 2003 I reported for Branch Manager at Tajganj, Agra branch and on 22 May 2003 relieved Mr. CP Sharma, Branch Manager for Zonal Office, Agra. Tenders for Renovation of Tajganj Branch opened at Zonal Office .From Friday 23 May 2003, I started working as Branch Manager.

On 7th June 2003 I was relieved for training at Hyderabad (program for Branch Managers Grade III and above from 9.06.2003 to 14.06.2003 at Bangerpet Staff College) and on Sunday, 8th June, due to the flight being delayed by 2 hours, reached Hyderabad at 10:45 PM .

For Bank Day 1st July 2003 two camps were organized one "Eye Camp" which started on 30th June 2003 at 11:30 AM with Dr. Aseem Agrawal and other doctors and the other "Senior Citizen Health Check Up Camp" which was Started on July 1, 2003 at 1:00 PM in which Dr. K. D. Arya and Dr. Dilip Soni conducted check up of visiting patients. Both the camps were very successful and people took full advantage.

In the Tajganj, Agra branch, I inherited such things, which took a long time to correct and a lot of hard work.

The first case was that of the Income Tax Department, who had issued a demand notice of a hefty amount (about 43 lakhs) citing the reason for not deducting TDS on the interest paid by the bank in the year 2000-2001 and repeatedly Was insisting for recovery. I got a summon from ITO (TDS) to appear before him on 15 September 2003, which had to be Adjourned because from 15 September to 18 September I had to go to Hyderabad for training. Afterwards I was called many times at income tax office and the commissioner pressurised to deposit some money. But I showed my inability. I engaged the entire staff to collect the old Form 15h and submit it to the Income Tax Department, which the ITO refused to accept. I took the services of CA Mr. Ankur Kumar Agrawal, who lives in Pratap Nagar and is a capable CA and filed an appeal against this demand. In the meantime another incident happened that the Commissioner called the Deputy General Manager at his office and somehow got deposited ? 50000 from him (by debiting Tajganj branch from other branch). I was informed later. I also appeared in the appeal on several dates and Commissioner ordered ITO to accept 15h forms which were submitted in the appeal, by the utmost diligence of CA Mr. Ankur Kumar Agrawal. Thus much of the demand was reduced. Later I was transferred and probably an appeal might have been filed again.

On 14th September 2003 reached Delhi by Shatabdi and on 15th September at 9:00 AM to Hyderabad.

On 16 September evening, visited Shri Simandhar Digambar Jain temple (House No. 158 /3-5-12, Street No. 6, Ramkot) . Lord 1008 Shri Shantinath, Shri Adinath, Shri Mahavirji and Shri 1008 Shri Simandhar ji are on the ground floor of the temple. On the first floor there are 24 Tirthankaras with Shri 1008 Shri Bharat-Adinath-Bahubali ji.

In the evening of 18 September, IA flight number IC 840 left for Delhi at 7:00 PM. Stayed in Delhi overnight and reached Agra in the morning of 19 September 2003.

Some staff at Tajganj branch pressurized me to give loan to their acquaintances which I refused.Angered by this, he asked a lot of people to write letters in which there were complaints against me for not giving loans. One person in front of whom letters were got written , told me the name of that staff member but I did not pay any attention .

Memories of SIB Agra Branch !

I was transferred from Tajganj branch to SIB Agra at the post of "Concurrent Auditor" . While working as Concurrent Auditor, I realized that this post is dumy post . Ignoring the deficiencies pointed out, the higher officials act on their own accord. I note there were serious irregularities in the accounts of a Firozabad unit in the branch. NPA accounts were deliberately not shown as NPAs. I made them aware many times and wrote to the general manager also. But all invain.The unit got best accomodatios for years together and at last declared NPA and the acoount got closed with nominal amount under compromise.Similarly I made several remarks against sanctioning a loan for "SLaughter HOUSE " but no heed was given to

my note .Loan sanctioned and became Cronic NPA withen subsequent years
.

Memories of main branch Agra!

After about 1 year, I was made a Concurrent Audit of SIB as well as Agra Main Branch and I had to audit 2 branches instead of 1.

Not only this, as per bank rules, I should get hometown before retirement, I was transferred to Bhogaon and was forced to stay on leave for many months because my wife's health was not allowing me to go. After some time she had to undergo major surgery of her head. It was also seen in the period that the union is also full of selfish elements. Work can be done only with the help of shovel. Despite having a fair case of mine, the union did not help and I myself wrote many letters to the general manager and asked for time to meet him by telephone, but did not get . In the end, I was transferred to Mathura instead of Bhogaon by some personal approach.

Memories of Mathura!

The RASECC/SAARC branch in Mathura was on the top floor of the main branch of State Bank of India. The NPA accounts of all the Mathura branches were followed up by SAARC. The NPA recovery position was very poor.

While living in Mathura, it became clear that there is a lobby working in State Bank of India, mainly in the Delhi circle, which is dominant. Whether that work is fair or unfair. They are capable to get desired work done against the rules, in many transfers and other inquiries etc.

On 31 July 2010, I was given farewell from Sarc Mathura and as it happens, all appreciated my working and behaviour . Because the union officials were also present in the farewell ceremony, I told this in very polite but firm wordsthat what should be the role of the union leaders and what is happening.

It will not be an exaggeration to say here that in the branches where I worked, most of the staff was cooperative and well received, due to which I could work smoothly. An emotional farewell letter was given to me by a daughter Richa from the last branch RASECC which is given below.

After completing
successful 3 Decades in
Bank. Now its the time to
start 2nd innings. But before
the time shades the line b/w
us I want to say that all your
colleagues will miss your optimistic
affectionate and benevolent nature

We'll try to fragrant
Just like U

From-
Richa &
RASECC. Mathu

4

My Better Half Smt. Sushma Jain !

My Beloved wife Sushma who left me alone !

Thunderclap (VAJRAPAT) !

23 February 2020

Day: Sunday 10:00 AM

Coming back from temple I straight to Sushma who had some anxiety. When I asked her, let's go to the hospital ! She wrapped her register (in which she was writing the Namokar mantra) and other items like a towel,pens etc. handed over to Ritu (son's wife) to keep in the cupboard and said that She will take it back after returning from the hospital. Childre may spoil the things. Son Vivek had gone to pick up Dr. Anupam Sharma from his house and doctor asked that he had taken a bath and would put on his clothes and just ready to come. One day earlier in the night, I called Neeraj when Sushma's health deteriorated. Neeraj Pankaj (Elder Brothers Sons) both came and get the oxygen Lavel checked by getting oxygen and BP machine from home. Oxygen level was low.

Neeraj immediately called Dr Anupam Sharma and he advised him to get admitted to Lotus Hospital.

Took out the wheelchair to be carried and checked the oxygen level again before leaving, it was fine.

It was 11:30 in the night, so I suggested to take her the next day in the morning. Maybe this was the mistake. Due to stomach pain in the night, I gave the medicine sent by Neeraj at 5:00 AM. Around 6:30 AM I prepared tea and gave it to Sushma and afterwords I went to the temple.

I checked the oxygen again at around 11:00, it was fine. Ritu fed him some porridge and I started checking oxygen and BP. When BP's machine gave ERROR twice, at first I thought there was something wrong with the machine, but when I looked at Sushma's face after that, she was dead. The eyes were slightly open and her soul/pran had passed through her eyes.

Immediately called Vivek back. I called Makhan (employee) upstairs from the office, put Sushma on a wheel chair, brought her down by lift and kept her in the car and took her to Saket Hospital where doctors declared her dead. By then Neeraj, Pankaj, Priyanka and Nitin ji had arrived. Priyanka took them to Pushpanjali Hospital but to no result. After returning, her dead body was laid on a sheet outside the office. A few hours later, the container for dead body from the Bajaja committee arrived. Sushma's body was shifted to it.

As the information spread, acquaintances and relatives started coming. Amit, Neeru from Delhi and Kuldeep, Neetu from Jaipur could come quite late and after their arrival, the process of donating Sushma's eyes was completed. And at around 6:30 PM, Sushma was taken to the electric crematorium, Tajganj, Agra, where she was cremated, and I thus dedicated my consort Sushma to fire and separated myself forever. What a heart-wrenching seen. robbed.

It is certain that as long as I live, I will not be able to forget Sushma's memories, her gratitude, her support and the moment I lived with her for 49 years.

Because Panchak was there in those days, so as per the orders of Acharya Shri 108 Shri Vasunandi Maharaj Ji, four coconuts (shriphal) were kept separately at the cremation ground, with the resolution that they would cooperate with her in the worship recitation.

Memories after Seperation !

Although there was no day after Sushma's departure, when she is not remembered. In the initial days, I thought that I will not live more than 3 months that's why I stopped shaving / hair cutting.

But when three months have passed and I remained alive, I got shaved and hair cutting.

While worshiping in front of God I feel her sitting near me as if she is also worshiping with me. Still on some prticular days when her memories got me weeped ,some lines have got written from my soul.

23.08.2020 Sunday!

Who will hold hands now?

Seeing a photo with Sushma in which she is holding my hand, a thought came to my mind that now who will hold my hand?

Today it has been 6 months since you left. Today is the same date and day Sunday when you left.

It is a coincidence that the Paryushan festival is starting from today and today is the day of best forgiveness.

You must be doing vandana worship in Nandishwar Dweep and Videha Kshetra. I wish that in the next festival I could accompany you.

28 September 2020 Monday!

Somewhere in my dream in the morning, I saw a temple. It was raining heavily. After a while, Sushma was also seen holding the wall and getting wet in the rain. I have said something but now I am not recollecting. I am not able to understand the meaning of dream.

3 October 2020 Saturday! Death of Bhabhiji Smt Jinendra Kumari Jain !

Today respected sister-in-law(Bhabhi ji) Mrs. Jinendra Kumari Jain passed away at 5:00 PM. since 1960 till now, brother and sister-in-law brought me up like their son.At 7:15 in the evening, had been taken to the electric crematorium Tajganj Agra for the last rites and in a short time, like Sushma, she too was dedicated to the fire. I'm feeling helpless.

Due to the Corona period, the program of Uthawani was done at home on 4th October with Namokar Mantra recitation and on 16th October at Jaipur

House Shantinath Digambar Jain Temple under the guidance of Bhura Panditji, Shanti Path was organized.

23 October 2020 Friday!

It's been 8 months since Sushma passed away today. I can't do anything except remembering.

Today went for darshan of Acharya Shri 108 Shri Vasundi Ji Gurudev in Bolkheda with Neeraj Pankaj .When Ch Gungun asked Acharyshree that BABA (my self)remains sad after the demice of Dadi (Sushma)he said to let me Stay busy. When this episode came again in the evening, he said that after the separation of a life partner, a person becomes like a living corpse. And I feel so.

14 November 2020 Saturday!

Today is Deepawali. For the first time without Sushma, Deepawali is looking strange. I got darshan at Jaipur House temple in the morning after a long time. Visiting the temple was almost stopped from March 2020 due to Corona. Lord Mahavir Nirvana Ladoo will be Tomorrow Dated 15.11. 2020 so our Diwali will be tomorrow.

15 November 2020 Sunday!

Arrived today around 10:00 AM to offer Ladoo. I offered Ladoo after reading poojan and Nirvana Kand. But Sushma was missing. Although Sushma is with me while offering Ladoo, imagined that she offered Ladoo. By the way, "Sushma is with us". I always do kalpana(imagine) in worship / chanting. I can not say how much more time will have to be spent alone.

Received information today, Acharya Shri 108 Shri Gyan Sagar ji had gone to Devlok in the evening. He was doing Chaturmas in Bara (Rajasthan). After Guru Bhakti in the evening, suddenly passed away to Devoka. Very sad news. Initiation ofAcharya Shri.as Muni took place on the day of Mahavir Jayanti and the movement to Devlok also happened on the day of Mahavir Jayanti.

19 November 2020 Thursday!

Today is our wedding anniversary . Had Sushma been alive, it would have been 49 years. Only memories are left. Today at around 5:15 AM, Sushma ji appeared with her brother Shri Surya Prakash Jain in a dream. Took me to a room on the terrace where the beds were lying. There was a strong gust of wind coming from a window. I told Sushma that it was cold , she smiled but didn't say anything.

At the same time, in another dream, a procession is probably going on in a bus. In that elder brother Late Shri Bhagwan Swaroop Jain Ji and Sushma's brother Manoj from Tundla are seen. And today message of death of Shri Arun Kumar Jain (Po Po) son Shri Chandra Prakash Jain received from Tundla. There is any corelation with the dream Can't say.

20 November 2020 Friday!

While looking at Sushma's cupboard, I found a small bag in which Sushma had collected the letters written by her and me. There was no opportunity to read those letters again in her lifetime. Today put all the letters in a file. There are letters in itSince 1971 till 1983. Reading the letters brought back old memories, but it was also sad that the one who could not bear my separation for a few days / months, went away after separating me forever. 3 days later 9 months will be completed. In seconds out of sight forever.

With Sushma- Only Memories remained !

29 November 2020 Sunday!

This morning after 5:00 o'clock I dreamed that we (all the family) are buying gold jewellary. I have a thick necklace in my hand and everyone has some jewelery in their hand. Sushma is also with me. On coming home, Sushma is sitting and saying that I had to buy clothes for winter too. I said we will go again tomorrow.

23.05.2021 Sunday!

Today it has been 15 months since Sushma gone , today is also Sunday like on23 February 2020 when she had left me alone.

Where have you gone?

Since 19 November 1971 onwards

till the morning of 23 February 2020

without ever asking

you didn't go anywhere

Even till morning on 23rd February 2020

didn't say anything

that you have to go

And

Did not tell even after my returning from temple

But suddenly at 11:00

Gone forever without telling / asking!

had something to say

what was the urgent work / what was my fault

because of

without telling

suddenly gone

That too forever!

Now I can only speculate

That

must have made such a big mistake

That's why you left!

I agree that you are very grateful to me,

I hurt you (in mind, word, body),

Cheated you too (by not fulfilling the promises made to you in your lifetime)

Apologies for all!

Be happy wherever you are!

I am trying to make promises made to you,

In which construction of Jain temple, Gaushala etc.

get completed before end of my life

I will never be happy without you!
your's
Jain sa'b!

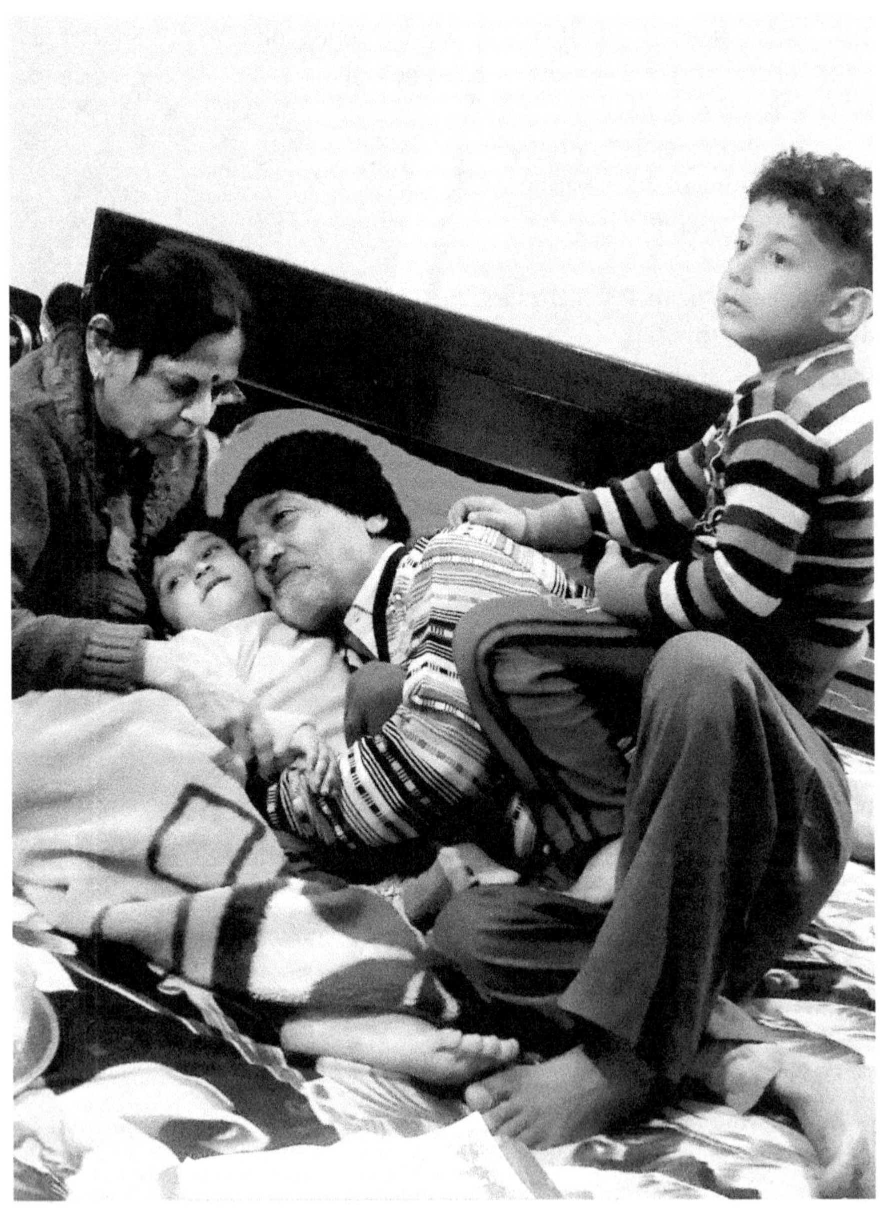

Sushma with Grand Children !

July 19, 2021 was my birthday and even after refusing, the children made a program to celebrate the birthday. After this I wrote on WhatsApp that there was no justification for celebrating the birthday without Sushma. In this context, Mrs. Sangeeta Jain wife Mr. Rajesh Kumar Jain (Daughter of Shri KCJain Saheb) forwarded a poem written by Major (Dr.) Shalini Singh , which is presented. I got a bit comfort by by reading it.

Greetings, Mama ji, your support means a lot to us.

Today I got a poem from somewhere I like to tell you.

title of poem(The poem is Hindi Language ,is reproduced below-Translation in ENGLISH followed)

"मरेजानेकेबाद"

जसि रात मदूँ ल ूँ आँख अपनी

और न फरि मेरी सुबह हो

होगंी ंजर्रू आँखें नम तमु्हारी

पर बहुत न तमु दखुी हो

मेरी हँसती तस्वीर टाँग देना

तमु हर कमर ें में

साथ दखिर्ूँी तमु्हें में

घर के हर कोन ें में

सुबह जाओग ें जब बाहर

हँस के वदिा कर्ूँी तमु्हें

शाम लौटोग ें जब थक कर

इंतजार करती मलिर्ूँी में

मेरी तस्वीर प ें न तमु

फूल माला चढा़ना

नही ं हूँ में साथ तमु्हार ें

खदु को याद न दलिाना

जब मलिकर बैठोग ें साथ

इक कुर्सी खा़ली रख लेना

में भी शामलि हूँ गपशप म ें

मन म ें यह यकीन कर लेना

सनुाना चटुकुल ें मझु ें

बेआवाज साथ हँस्ूँी में

पहले सुना है मैंने
यह भी नहीं कहूँगी मैं
जैसे बात करते हो मुझसे आज
कल भी वैसे ही करना
मैं हूँ तुम्हारे आस पास
इस बात का यकीन रखना
मुझसे करते हो गर प्यार
इक दूजे का रखना खयाल
अगर दुखा दिल किसी का भी
दुखी होंगी तुम्हारे साथ मैं भी
मेरी याद को बोझिल न बना लेना
मेरा नाम लेकर जरा मुस्कुरा देना
न दिखूँ तुम्हें तो मूँदे लेना आँखें
अपने भीतर मुझे साथ पा लेना
तुम्हारी हँसी में खिलखिलाऊँगी मैं भी
तुम्हारी खुशी में खुश हो जाऊँगी मैं भी
जीना जिंदगी को हर घड़ी भरपूर तुम
तुम्हारे साथ जीती जाऊँगी मैं भी
-मेजर (डा) शालिनी सिंह

Translation of poem :
"after I leave"
The night I close my eyes
and it's not my morning again
Surely your eyes will be moist
but you should not very sad
hang my laughing picture
you in every room
I'll see you with me
in every corner of the house
when you go out in the morning
will send you off with a laugh
Will come back in the evening when tired
I will wait
not you on my picture
garlanding flowers
I'm not with you

don't remind yourself
when you sit together
lay down a chair
I am also involved in gossip
make sure of it
tell me jokes
I will laugh with voiceless
I've heard before
I wouldn't even say
as you talk to me today
do the same tomorrow
i'm around you
be sure of
do you love me
take care of each other
If anyone's heart hurts
I will be sad with you too
don't burden my memory
smile on my name
If I don't see you, then close your eyes
get me inside you
I will smile in your laughter too
I will be happy in your happiness too
Live life full of you every moment
I will win with you
-Major (Dr) Shalini Singh

19.11. 2021 Friday!

Today is our wedding anniversary. If Sushma was alive today, she would have been celebrating 50th anniversary. Now there are only tears in my eyes and only memories of Sushma are left.

3 November 2021 Wednesday!

Today is Dhanyateras / Chaturdashi, Choti Deepawali. Tomorrow is Deepawali. Missing Sushma. I don't know how long I have to live like this.

Mrs. Ratna prabha Jain, sister, passed away 2 days before the festival. Her memories are also there. I was hoping for some miracle. As she used to tell that she had died in childhood and when she reached the top she saw a beard person saying to other why did you bring her .She is yet to live, they pushed her from there. She got alived.

4ᵗʰ November 2021 Thursday!

Today is Deepawali. Today none of my ancestors is alive. Grandparents, parents, brothers and sisters have all gone away. I am alone. How long to carry this body, I don't know.

Today, Ladoo was offered on the occasion of Nirvana Mahotsav of Lord 1008 Shri Mahavir Swami, at Shri 1008 Shri Shantinath Digambar Jain Temple , Teachers Colony, Jaipur House, Agra.

Worship of Lord Mahavir Swami and Shri Gautam Swami by Muni Shri 108 Shri Sudhasagar ji from 1:30 to 4:30 PM, at Chandkhedi temple ji with 64 lamps, which was broadcasted on Jinvani channel and worshipedat home.

In the evening, lit Deepaks at the temple and chaityalaya at Teachers Colony /Jaipur House . After returning from there, went to Sunita's residence where all the family members including Pankaj Neeraj were present. It was Sunita's first Diwali after the death of Shri Ajit Kumar.

Sushma in dreams

2ⁿᵈ January 2022 Sunday!

Met Sushma in a dream tonight. I am in some other house. I have to go somewhere. She is asking whether it will be visible from below. I said don't worry, I will take you upstairs. She seems satisfied with this. Some children are studying outside the house. I have gone to the room and some people are visible from there also.

7ᵗʰ January 2022 Friday!

Today Babbu (Priyanka) has seen Sushma in a dream dressed in very beautiful clothes making something in the kitchen (118 Manas Nagar). Also seen many pomegranates on a pomegranate tree in the house. Also seen a pig entered inside the house.

8 January 2022 Saturday!

This morning ,in a dream,we are staying in a hotel and preparing to leave for the airport. Neeraj is giving a Bislery bottle of water to a child. I am tickling Sushma that earlier went to Port Blair and now going here.

29 January 2022 Saturday!

I have seen Sushma in my dream tonight. Gas is burning.She is preparing to cook something. Sushma is happy nearby but did not talk.

30 January 2022 Sunday!

Have seen Sushma tonight too but can't remember the dream.

Although it is said:

Memories makes a person miserable!

But even after many efforts, neither the memories are fading nor I am able to forget her !

In such a situation, it seemed appropriate that I should compile his memories in the form of a story.

So I am trying to bring alive the forgotten memories which are in my mind.

Sushma Katha / My Better Half Sushma jain !

Sushma was not only wife for me. She was an advisor,supporter,well wisherand everything which I required.Almost 49 years of our union lost in a jiffy. How she helped me in every step in every situation, nobody knows except me.

In today's time it is rare if not impossible to find such a wife.

It was her sacrifice and Vatsalya (affection), due to which the two families remained like one family and she stood by the family in every odd situation. She remained fully active and despite the disability in one leg, she continued to do household work as well as market with full devotion.

From where do I start her story? After marriage on 19 November 1971, he came to Agra and maintained harmony in the family in every way. At that time the family was living on rent at 26/67, Ahir Pada Raja Mandi Agra.

It is said that the importance of a person is known only after his departure, but I came to know the importance of Sushma only after few years of marriage.

On the first day after marriage, I told her that Bhai Saheb and Bhabhi ji raised me like their own child from childhood and any lack in their respect would be the cause of my sorrow. She kept it in mind for ever and Fulfilled till last moment. Financial conditions of the family were bad from the beginning. My mother Mrs. Mahadevi Jain and father Mr. Har prasad ji had died within 1 week. The house expenses were met by the salary of Bhagwan Swaroop ji (MD Jain was as a teacher in Inter College).

Probably in 1969, there was a Jain annual fair in Awagarh of Etah district, when Sushma's family members proposed my marriage to Sushma at the place of Shri Gulabchand Jain (Sushma's maternal uncle) in Awagarh through sister-in-law's father Shri Jagdish Prasad Jain.

Seen Sushma at Shri Gulab Chand ji's shop, and decided to get married despite having her polio in one leg. This decision was probably my good fortune.

On this day before the Rath Yatra, we had a bid for Shantidhara of 1008 Shri Bhagwan Pushpdant Ji Maharaj along with Bhai Saheb Shri Bhagwan Swaroop ji.

I don't remember many things after that.

There was a ceremony on 17.10.1971,when Sushma's father Shri Jayanti Prasad Jain and other relatives came with Pandey Shri Ugrasen Jain ji from Tundla and in the ceremony, they put ? 5000 cash , some clothes and fruits etc on my hand as a token of engagement . There are no other memories regarding wedding. Only one incident is there that on the morning of the wedding procession, tea was being made in which sugar was added twice and the tea became too sweet.

It is also remembered that the procession stayed at Tundla square in Dharamshala and was for 3 days. The second day picture was seen in the Prasad Picture Palace Hall.

The Barat went on Wednesday 17-11-1971 (Margashirsha Amavasya) married on 18-11-71 (Margashirsh Shukla Paksha Pratham) and departed on 19-11- 1971 (Margashirsha Shukla Paksha II)

After coming to Agra on 19-11 -1971, in the daily routine was to wake up before sunrise, to go for worship with sister-in-law at Shri Digambar Jain Parasnath Mandir Raja ki Mandi Agra, regularly and after returning working with sister-in-law under her guidance.

In addition to cooking, the main activities of that time were:

Refining of wheat, cereals, pulses etc.

- Breaking stone coals (for cooking on firewood) and making laddus to burn them with powder

- Scrubbing dry utensils (by ashes)

To prepare various types of sweets, snacks for home use and guests.

- Laundry (by hand) Drying and pressing of clothes

-Preparing lunch boxes for children and siblings

- sewing clothes

-Setting soap in a bucket for washing clothes

- sweeping the house, cleaning, dusting

In all these works, along with sister-in-law, Sunita's cooperation was also there.

No matter how late she slept in the night, but getting up by 5:00 in the morning and after bath etc. to reach the temple at the time of Abhishek, it was a daily task.

And thus the time was spent in Raja ki Mandi. Although I was trying for a job for a long time, but after the arrival of sushma, on 23 February 1972, the efforts of Shri Ashok Kumar Jain (brother of sister-in-law) at State Bank of India Agra City branch. I got the job of Temporary Cashier. At that time

Mr. KK Sharma Union Secretary, Mr. LN Goyal Agent/Branch Manager and Mr. Kunwar Lal Jain (Owner of OswaL Emporium/Tour Aids) was Head Cashier in Agra City Branch.

I remember an incident from the first day in the bank. In the evening, in the chest (treasury) notes of 100 and above were checked with clip system, some notes were folded in the pile by the head cashier and we counted the rest of the notes and noted them. By adding them the head cashier used to make sure that there are 100 notes in the packet. I counted all notes including folded ones which cause them laughed and then they told me that the folded notes were not counted.

After this, learned the complete work in a week, including to make currency chest slip.

Life was going well after Sushma's arrival in Agra Brother Saheb MD Jain Inter College used to go to Hari Parvat Agra to teach and Chiranjeev Sunita, Vinita, Pranita used to study in Shri Digambar Jain School Raja Mandi. On the occasion of my marriage, Pankaj used to study for about one and a half years. and younger sister Mrs. Ratan Prabha Jain and brother-in-law Mr. Kunwar Bahadur ji Jain's younger son Barbie (Rajiv) was 14 days old! b Sushma was very skilled in sewing embroidery knitting and after marriage the first sweater was knitted for Barbie. Chiranjeev Sunita She had a great interest in sewing embroidery and had learned a lot from Sushma.

Although I married Sushma without any greed or demand, with feeling of someone's happiness with my cooperation.But this could not be accepted by the society and relatives. Everyone thought that I must have taken big money/property to marry the handicapped.

The relatives exaggerated about Sushma's family as one of the nobles of Tundla and was in a position to give a lot.

The fact was that Sushma's Baba Shri Sheo Prasad Jain was actually a nobleman and there were only three or four families in Tundla who had a Cluster of Houses. And he was one of them.

Shri Sheo Prasad ji had two marriages. From first wife Sushma's father Shri Jayanti Prasad ji was born and from second wife four sons Shri Jinendra Prasad, Jitendra Prasad, Jaswant Prasad, Jasvir Prasad and two daughters Smt. Kusum Jain and Smt. Aruna Jain.

According to the father's wish from the father's property, all the brothers got almost equal property. A very big house is situated in Station Road, Tundla, in which there is arrangement for the living of all the brothers along with their families. There were six brothers of Sushma (Shri Chandra

Prakash Jain, Shri Surya Prakash Jain, Shri Gyan Prakash Jain, Shri Dhyan Prakash Jain, Shri Manoj Prakash Jain and Shri Anuj Prakash Jain) and two sisters Smt. Shailesh Jain and Smt. Sushila Jain. Financial condition of Sushma's father Shri Jayanti Prasad ji Jain was not very good. It was because of the big family and lack of employment/earnings.

But being from the family of a noble man, everyone considered him to be rich. Although he also had enough houses and land, he had nothing in his hands due to the rift in the family. The reality of Sushma's family's condition was known after a long time. Due to the exaggerations by relatives, a feeling also developed in me that due to non-demanding, I was harmed and due to this confusion, I started distant living with them and as such Sushma did not go to Tundla much.

Sushma's three brothers were married before my marriage. Shri Chandra Prakash Jain was married to Raja Ka Taal (Firozabad) and his wife was called by the name of Taal Wali. No business could be successful to Shri Chandra Prakash Jain . The second brother Mr. Surya Prakash Jain was married to Mrs. Veena Jain of Shikohabad. His social and economic status was good as he was an IOW in the Railways and later retired as an executive engineer. Sushma had lived with her in many places in her childhood. The name of one place was Ghatera, which is possibly around Jhansi. This was told by Sushma.

The third brother, Mr. Dhyan Prakash, was related to Barhan. Initially, he was sitting with his father at a cement shop and later worked as an accountant (bookkeeper) at various places in Agra. Later shifted to Delhi where his daughter is working.

The other 3 brothers Mr. Gyan Prakash, Mr. Manoj Prakash and Anoj Prakash were all married from Firozabad and all engaged in different business in Tundla.

Sushma was well when she was about 6 months old. Suddenly her health deteriorated and one leg was affected by polio. There was a lot of treatment and finally two or three operations were done in AIIMS Delhi but the leg could not be completely cured and In such a situation, she could not continue her study . It was learned from Sushma that she did not have many friends because after school the condition of going to college could not be made. I remember the names of 1-2 of her friends, one of whom was Ms. Durga Tiwari and Ms. Kusum Chouhan , though his aunt Mrs. Aruna Jain and uncle's daughter Pinni and an uncle's brother-in-law's daughter Ms. Mridula Jain of Shikohabad were also like her friends. But after marriage, I had not many meetings/conversations with any of them.

Sushma's attitude was cooperative from the beginning. Large family and low income also also could not get her annoyed and she never complained for anything and lived in harmony in the family. It was in her habit not to refuse any work. Preparing young children for school , putting their lunch boxes, making girls' peaks, etc., used to complete all the work with affinity. An incident about this was told by Pranitha that in her childhood she used to go to school after getting her braid made. When she was sleeping, Sushma cut her hair to a short. When she came to know about this, she cried a lot and Sushma only persuaded her and kept her quite.

And thus the wheel of time kept running and in 1972 Sushma became pregnant. On the same time sister-in-law also became pregnant. In June 1973 Neeru was born to Sushma on 27th June and Neeraj to Bhabhi ji on 26th June.

Due to two deliveries in the house , there was no one else to work in the house and the children were small. So brother-in-law's father-in-law, Shri Jagdish Prasad Ji Jain took both of them to Awagarh and both stayed there for about 40 days Since Neeraj and Neeru were brought together and at times when sister-in-law did not have milk, Sushma used to feed Neeraj with her milk throuh her breast.

Due to low income, it was not easy to maintain such a large family, yet the house was running with Sushma's understanding and cooperation. One thing is appreciated that Sushma never complained that she had any problem. In the evening She always used to wait for my returning from bank and waited to takefood.

In October 1974, I was deputed to State Bank of India Staff Training Centre, 49, Prabhat Nagar, Saket, Meerut for one month training. Neeru as a child used to miss me. In a letter to me, as narrated by Sushma in her letter to me. Deepawali was falling in the middle of training and I had to come on Deepawali. I went to Agra with great pleasure but did I know that as soon as I arrived I would be greeted by a very sad news. My younger brother-in-law, Shri Kunwar Bahadur Jain was reported to have died in a tractor accident and on the day of Diwali, Bhai Saheb, Bhabhi Ji, Sushma and I first reached Etah by bus and from there to Phaphotoo where there was a very disheartening scene.

After returning from Phaphotoo, took 1 day leave (although leave is not available during training but leave was approved in special circumstances) . After the marriage of Didi in 1960, brother-in-law got employed in

Telephone Exchange, Ajmer in 1963. After training from Ajmer, Sujangarh, Sujangarh to Agra, Agra to Kasganj, Kasganj to Etah. Last posting was in Etah. When he went to Sujangarh, he had a daughter who died a few days after reaching Sujangarh.

Sister-in-law had come to Raja Mandi's house (Mr. Bengali Mal jain's house which we used at rent) with that daughter. Sister told that there was some problem in the house which we had taken on rent in Sujangarh.On transfer from there as soon as they left the house, the gate closed automatically and a lot of crows gathered around the house started making noise.

Due to posting in Etah, the family lived in the village Fafotu. That day brother-in-law went to Barhan to get the tractor and was bringing the tractor from Barhan. Nephew Kulli (Pradeep Jain) was with the tractor and came to Awagarh. On approaching, a woman asked them to let her sit on the tractor, for which Kulli refused .

After some time brother-in-law went to toilet and while returning, a boy of 14-15 years asked to sit on the tractor. This time also Kulli refused. But brother-in-law gave permission.

As soon as brother-in-law sat down, the driver asked about some stains on his face. He aske Kulli about it and suddenly all fell down as the bolts of the tractor broke. Everyone else got up. Brother-in-law couldn't get up.

People tried to stop many buses coming from Etah , so that he could be sent to Agra for treatment. But no bus stopped due to Diwali rush. Brother-in-law realized something and started asking to call sister again and again but this could not be possible he died . It's amazing that no one knows where had gone the boy .

Sister had 4 small children at that time. 3 sons, eldest Rajesh Kumar Jain (Raju) about 9 years, Sanjeev Kumar Jain about 7 years, Rajiv Kumar Jain (Borby) about 3 years and a daughter Mamta Jain approx. 5 years .

The money received from brother-in-law's fund and life insurance money was deposited in the bank by Brother-in-law's uncle Shri Parmeshwari Dayal ji Jain and jijaji's Brother-in- law Shri Jinvardas Ji Jain in the form of FDR. It was spent in buying a house for Raju in Jhilmil Colony in Delhi and FDR of 25000 was given to Mamta on the occasion of marriage. Brother-in-law also had land but according to the law of that time or for any other reason, the name of sister was not got the land recordsand the kids sold all the land when they grew up.

Shree1008 Lord Parshwanath ji Mahua !

I went to Bharuch (Gujarat) along with brother-in-law Shri Abhay Kumar Jain (elder brother, Late Shri Kunwar Bahadur Jain) for marriage for my niece Chiranjeev Mamta (Daughter Late Shri Kunwar Bahadur Jain and Sister Shrimati Ratnaprabha Jain). And from there one day visited Mahua ji , where blessed with darshan of 1008 Lord Parshwanath with Abhishek-Puja. One incident remembered that Sushma packed puris and potato tomato curry (which was her special recipe) for dinner on the way. When I took out vegetables and puris, brother-in-law did not take vegetables and I thought that he would probably given up potatoes, as most of Jains do.But when asked he told that he has given up tomato because tomato comes in "Bahubijah"(having many seeds).

To increase income, in the year 1974, with the advice of Sushma, open a store in house number 26/67, it was named Pankaj Store.

While in Aligarh (With cash to Kasimpur)I used to live with Mr DBMathur of Agra. We both used to cook completely vegetarian food together. Once I had put plates of both for lunch and at the same time washerman came to collect clothes for press and looked the plates. On his departure, Mathursaheb told that you should have covered the plates , we should not show our meals to everyone.

Sushma kept green chili pickle which wer liked by everyone and I had to write to Sushma on 13.12. 1974, to prepare 1 kg of chilli pickle . I also ordered packets of lentil spice (in the name of Jagraj masala which was started by Shri Vinay Kumar Jain) from Awagarh.

In the letter of 16. 01. 1975, Sushma wrote sadly "Bhabhi ji has gone to Awagarh and there is no arrangements here. In the reply, I wrote to ask for money from Ashok for the time being and I got repaid.

Such situations may have arose many times, yet he did not complain.

The financial conditions were so bad that sometimes money had to be arranged by keeping Sushma's jewellery.

She used to get angry very quickly, which was inevitable. Nevertheless, in a letter dated 30.01.1975, she apologized by cursing her anger.

After this, in June 1975, I went to Hapur with cash and stayed till October 1975. In a letter dated June 7, 1975, he wrote, "Doing something for wife-children might be sin. Always do this. Let wife weeping" .At that time brother's health was bad and the doctor had aske for X-ray etc. So I gave money to sister-in-law and could not give it to Sushma. Later, Sushma and Neeru were also taken to Hapur. Sushma was pregnant for the second time.

I was taking a room in the house ofShri CB Sharma ji, who was working in the bank itself.Sharma ji was a goodperson and his family members also respectful.

In a house opposite to Sharma ji's house ,a subordinate employee of the bank was living who used to come almost every night after drinking liquor and beating his wife. The wife's screams were heard and looked very strange.

An incident of Hapur. One day three or four sadhus came with elephants and asked to get Neeru (daughter of 2years old) to sit on the elephant. I, with Sushma's consent, made Neeru sit on an elephant. As soon as she sat down, the sadhu was not ready to take her down and started asking for money. Neeru started crying. After giving 100 -150 rupees. Neeru got down and happily run to Sushma.

I left Sushma in Agra in August 1975 and Neetu was born on 6 September 1975.

Smt Neetu Jain with Husband Shri Kuldeep Jain !

In March 1975, an article came out in Sarita for the treatment of orthopedics, in which Dr. Pramod Kumar Sethi (PK Sethi) who was in Sawai Mansingh Hospital, Jaipur, was well praised. I noted his address in my diary and thought of treatment of Sushma.

Went to Dhampur with cash in December 1975 and stayed till February 1976.

The Branch Manager in Dhampur was Mr. Tekchand ji and a clerk (name I don't remember) used to call himself junior JN Kapoor.Once there had some conflict between Branch Manager and Union member. The BM called the police . An Aryaka Mataji 105 Mrs. (Name is not remembered) was seated in Dhampur Jain temple and she had special affection for me. Probably there was some sacrament/relation of previous birth. This was also said by Sushma. When I came back from Dhampur , she came to drop me at the station and she had tears in her eyes. I couldn't understand her affection. She gave me some books, including two parts of Mahavir Vani, written by Rajneesh.

Shri Vishnoi ji was the chief cashier in Dhampur and was a very friendly person. His father was not there and Mother and his wife lived at home.Their relations were not harmonious. He used to come daily from Najibabad. He once said that while reaching home , his wife and mother both complain of each other . But I satisfy/ get dsolution by explaining both separately. I note that in Dhampur, I and Vijay Kumar Garg, used to take cold water bath and had breakfast of Bread butter . Apart from breakfast I also used to eat bread and butter. Its effect was that I fell ill after returning from Dhampur. One Jain family in Dhampur helped me a lot .They used to send Dalia etc during my illness .I can't remember his name now, but he had come to visit Agra once and I was not here, so he reached Tundla.

There is also rememberance of a clerk in Dhampur, Mr. RK Jain, who once came to Agra with children.

In 1976-77, Umesh (Mama ji's son) ran away from Awagarh. Searched for him a lot. Asked many pundits but no result. On one day, in the morning from Agra Cantt, two GRP soldiers took him home. Everyone was surprised. I came to know that he had come from Mumbai without ticket and was caught at Cantt. He gave my reference to the policemen and told that I am in State Bank of India, so they brought him home. and left. I tried to pay some money to them but they refused. When asked Umesh about leaving , he did not give any satisfactory answer.

Umesh and his elder brother Prakash lived with their mother in Awagarh and worked as sweet merchants. Probably due to loss/inadequate income, he fled. Umesh was not getting any work at that time. Still, his name was got written in the employment exchange office and he knew the work of sweet merchant, so somehow at the time of staff-canteen in the Chhipitola branch of State Bank of India was taken over by the bank and by luck / trying, he got job in the canteen. Later he passed the High School and Inter examinations and took promotion in the clerical cadre. Now he too has retired and is leading a happy life with the children.

Sushma has written in the letter dated 25.05.1979 that Umesh Bhai Saheb was asking about clothes. I had written in reply that I will get him clothes after return .

Umesh was married on 23.11.1981 to Mrs. Sarla Jain, daughter of Mr. Madan Kumar Jain, resident of Barhan, and all the ceremonies including marriage were completed in 4, mini MIG, Friends Colony. At that time Shri KKAgrawal was Branch Manager at AGRA Branch who sent me congratulations. Out of the amount received at the time of cermony, I had deposited some amount in ADA for Umesh's house and he was allotted D-184 house in Kedar Nagar, Agra.

To increase the income of the family, Sushma bought a sweater knitting machine on 27/11/1977 but could not be much successful.

In the year 1981, on 24th September, the third daughter Priyanka Jain was born in Sakya Nursing Home in Agra. After some time of her birth, I moved the family to Etah and stayed there in the house of Mr. Saxena Saheb on Thandi Sarak.

During my stay in Pilua, I used to live in Etah with family and used to come from Pilua. In Etah, sister Smt Ratan Prabha Jain also lived with children, her younger sister-in-law Smt.Shrikanta also lived in the same house in her sister-in-law's house .In ouster room of the building lived a tea seller. In the upper floor lived his sister-in-law's family, in which Nandoi was Mr. Jinwar Das Jain and two sons Mr. Pradeep Jain and Subhash Jain.

At that time I had a small white colored puppy. One night when I went to my sister's place with the puppy, it started barking at the tea seller. The tea seller said how nice a puppy is.just after returning from there, Puppy fell ill at night and could not recover even after a lot of treatment.

Veterinary doctor in Pilua, Mr. Saxena Sahib himself came to see him and suppressed him. But after three-four days he died.

From the beginning it was my thinking that Sushma's disability should not be a cause of trouble in her old age and therefore I wanted that after my passing away , she should not have financial problems. No amount could be deposited in her name. Therefore ,I have extended my cooperation to Sushma, by registering Power of Attorney for House No. 4 Mini MIG, Friends Colony in her name so that she would not face any problem in future.

However She herself had to get this property registerd in the name of Smt Sonal Jain w/o.Neeraj Jain (niece) .The reason behind this was the forecastings by many "You will not be able to get this house vacated without a lawsuit", and not only me, Sushma also wanted that there should never be a conflict/ litigation among two families, including heirs of both the families.

Sushma had a lot of love for animals and birds. First of all, a puppy wastakenin Pilua died.In Shikohabad one German Shefard bitch Kimi was taken up by Bobby (Rajeev) who so mixed up in the family. Whenever we used to come to Agra by car from Shikohabad, Kimi was the first to sit in the car. When Kimi was young, Sushma used to bathe her in her lap and kept her lovingly. Coming from Shikohabad to Agra , she completely protect the house and many times guarded the house from thieves. Everyone was very sad on Kimi's death.

After kimi,Vivek brought a dog (German Shepherd) named Nodi. Sushma kept him with full care. wounded birds etc. if found ,got full treatment from Sushma till it got cured.

Nodi protected the house, family and Vivek a lot. A boy who lived like a domestic servant, entered the house one night and hid in the bathroom. Vivek came at 12:00 at night. Nody was pointing to the bathroom again and again. Vivek opened the bathroom door with a stick, then the boy came out and said I am. When asked to call police, he started crying and said that my father had a heart attack and he will die after hearing this news.

On 27 January 2013, Vivek brought a new puppy (Bull Machef), which was also named Nody .

On 18 .01. In 1986, a shop space (10' * 20') in Manas Nagar was purchased by Sushma from Prempuri Cooperative Society for Rs.15000.

On 09.01.1990 she bought a plot number 156 (200 Sq.Yards) in Avadhpuri and probably, since then only everything got sold out. Loan was approved for this house from LIC, But on the occasion of Diwali 2011, Chandra Sheel property Dealer got it sold at nominal price to Mr. Manohar Singh .Once I had refused but he called Neeraj and I had to sell.

Around the year 1983, I got a house put up in DDA in the name of Mr. Umesh Jain and the house got allotted at 22B, Jhilmil Colony. But after Vinita's marriage in the year 1986 I had to sell it at very cheap rate (which was taken by Mr. Rajesh Jain's uncle) as the marriage loans had to be repaid.

On 20 February 1984, son Vivek Jain was born in Shakya Nursing Home.

Vivek's birthday!

Vivek's fifth birthday!

At that time we did not have the knowledge that it is inauspicious and wrong to celebrate birthday by lighting candles because extinguishing cannot be a symbol of happiness. Similarly, cutting a cake is also inauspicious because cutting is also not a sign of happiness. Cutting / extinguishing, all this is the system of western culture and seeing them, we went on moving the wrong path. Worshiping God, lighting a lamp and feeding laddus is a symbol of happiness. One should also take the blessings of Gurus and senior people on this occasion.

Sushma was proficient in every task. She was the master in cooking. She used to make all kinds of recipes in minutes. I note that when I used to go from Agra to Aligarh, Awagarh, Deeg, Mathura, she would get up at 4:00 in the morning. Ist used to go to the temple with me and if I left at 6:30 after worshiping, then before that she used to prepare the entire lunch box (by keeping lentils, roti, rice, chutney and sweets).

Vivek Jain with wife Mrs. Ritu Jain.
In the year 1983, on September 5, Chiranjeev Sunita's marriage was confirmed with Mr. Ajit Kumar Jain, son of Mr. Om Prakash Jain, resident of Dibiyapur. Engagement ceremony took place on 17.04.1984 and marriage took place on 20.04.1984. Sushma's special role was there , in Sunita's marriage . Due to not having enough money for the wedding, Sushma had asked to give ,recently taken double bed and wardrob, for her own use a couple of days ago, to Sunita's wedding and gave . Sushma's brother Mr. Surya Prakash Jain also attended the wedding.He had some relationship with them. We had given only rings, utensils and clothes at the door. Sunita's father-in-law got angry and asked Surya Prakash ji that there should be a chain also.Thus put the demand for chain. Due to lack of money, Sushma took out the money received for Vivek (Vivek was two months old at that time and Sushma had kept aside the money received to him since birth) and gave it to me to purchase the gold chain. On the day of departure, before departure, I went to the market and brought the gold chain and handed it over to father -in-law of Sunita.
In the year 1986, on 27th April, Vinita's marriage got confirmed with Mr. Jinesh Jain son of Mr. Manohar Lal Jain Firozabad. This program was concluded at the Lal Mandir in Delhi where I, Bhai Saheb, Bhabhi Ji and Sushma had reached. 12.11.1986 was the date for engagement ceremony . The wedding ceremony was held during the day on 17.11.1986 and vidai at around 7:00 in the evening.

On October 3, 1992, in the park of Awadhpuri Colony, with the permission of the committee, the construction of Jain temple was started. There were plots of Shri Ashok Kumar ji, Chakresh Jain Firozabad, wife Sushma Jain and half-completed houses were also built, but Everyone sold their houses. Therefore the temple could not be built and Vaishno Mandir was built by other people at that place and in the remaining part of the park is used for the transformer of electricity departmentand the police post /chowki.

Around year 1990, Pankaj, Neeraj got the agency of Goldie Spices . Though this business was not bad but due to supply of goods on credit, got a good money blocked and could not succeed as the company used to send the goods only after taking money in advance.

In the year 1997, according to the wish of Neeraj, an NBFC company was registered in the name of Shri Parswa Finvest Ltd. In the registration of the company, Mr. RK Gupta, Chartered Accountant, brother of Dr. B.K.Gupta, helped a lot. He himself went to Kanpur for regitration under companies Act. During working in the company, the guidelines of Reserve Bank of India got changed and only rated company from Cricil could take deposits from public. So this work could not go long.

In the meantime, Pankaj started the work of providing cable connections in the name of Shubham Cable in both Friends Colony and Manas Nagar.

On January 28, 1995, Praneeta's marriage was fixed with Mr. Vinay Kumar Jain, Firozabad, and on February 18, 1995, the marriage took place in Manas Nagar, in the park in front of our house, and I remembered Praneeta's father-in-law 's remark"Vijay Swarup ji , you have got such a big pandal built". On 26 February 1995, inUma Marriage Complex (Currently CTV Office) Ladies Sangeet was organized. The arrangements for food etc, in all the programs were done by Mr. Rakesh Kumar Halwai (near Chitra Talkies).

We alongwith Neeru went to Yamuna Vihar ,Delhi, on 27.09.1995 for a formal meeting with the family of Shri Amit jain at 10:00 a.m. at Rishabh Vihar Mandir. On 3rd Nov. 1995 went to Yamuna Vihar Delhi to engage Amit Jain .At that time Mr. Kailash Chand Jain (Chiranjeev Sangeeta's father) was also with us. The engagement took place on 5th November 1995 and the marriage took place on 14 February 1997 in Delhi.

A very sad incident happened after the engagement. Neeru's father-in-law Mr. Mahesh Chand Jain, who had left for Delhi from here after engagement , very happily on 5th night driving the car himself, passed away of heart attack in the evening on 6th November 1995. On 7th Nov when we received this news all were astonished. Immediately we (Bhai Saheb, Bhabhi Ji, Me, Sushma) went to Delhi, but by then everything was over.

Engagement of Neeru and Amit at AGRA !

Shri Mahesh Chandra ji was a very jolly and talkative person and because of him this relationshipcould be managed.

We went to Delhi on 14 February 1997 for marriage of Neeru and Amit from Agrasen Bhawan in Delhi Vivek Vihar.

Pankaj was married to Mrs. Chhaya Jain on 3rd May 1997 at Khandelwal Bhawan Shahganj Agra.

Chiranjeev Sukirta got married to Mr. Pawan Jain, of Etah , on 4th May 1997 from Uma Marriage Complex (currently CTV Office), Manas Nagar.

Neetu's son Sanskar was born on 23 September 2000 at Shakya Nursing Home in Agra. I was in Jhunjhunu. This information was received from Neeraj.

28 December 2000 Thursday!

Bought a car (Indica DLE) in the name of Sushma Jain today from Ashok Auto Sales, Sanjay Place, Agra.

Chiranjeev Priyanka Jain's marriage was fixed with Mr. Nitin Jain son of Mr. Padam Chand Jain, Belanganj Agra on20.02.2005 and marriage on 5 May 2005, at Shree Agrasen Bhawan (Upper Floor), Water Works, Agra.

In the year 2012, the marriage of Chiranjeev Vivek was finalised with Mrs. Ritu Jain, daughter of Mr. Satyendra Jain, resident of Firozabad. Marriage on June 17.2012 from Hotel Grand and On June 18, 2012, Ladies Sangeet program was held in the CTV office premises.

Offering Shrifal to Lord Shri 1008 Shri Shantinath Bhagwan on the
occasion of marriage !

Some memories from the occasion of Vivek's wedding !

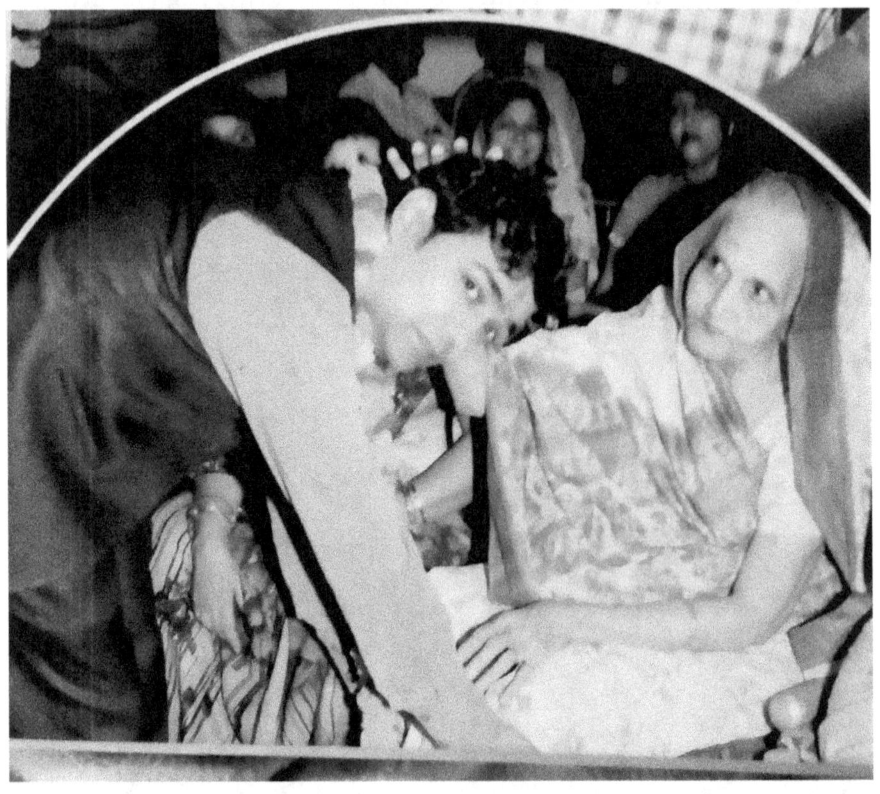

Some memories from the occasion of Vivek's wedding !

In the year 2013, on 19th August, Vivek-Ritu's son Arjit was born and Sushma got the opportunity to play with the grandson. In April 2013, Neeraj had a daughter Gracey. Sushma could not go to the hospital to see her and went to join the program of 6th day (Chhati)at 4, Pandav Nagar. After returning from there, she slipped while climbing in the night and got a slight fracture in the leg.

After that she almost stopped going to the temple. A lift was also installed for her convenience. From the lift, she used to get down in a wheelchair, and used Car for going to temple .Had Darshan from outside the temple. She also used to go to the temple in the evening for listening "Bhaktavar Path"while sitting in the car. But gradually the condition of her feet got very bad and ultimately established on the bed. and used to observe

Jinvani channel and Paras channel, whichare the main channels of Jainism. On 16 June 2016 daughter Pihoo was born to Vivek-Ritu and everyone got an opportunity to play with her. Sushma had a special attachment to Pihoo and Pihoo, after coming from school, used to take meals from the hands of Dadi and got slept in Amma's lap .She still haven't forgotten Amma and start weeping any time for her. Many memories are in her mind. Once both Pihoo and Arjit purchased Gas Baloons and got them free in the air after writing their names as messages for their Ammaji saying that Amma will get it.

Sushma went to Shri Mahavirji in May 2019 for Pihu's hair cut which was her last visit to any pilgrimage. Went to Delhi in January 2020 for Ankit's (son of Smt Vinita and Shri Jinesh Kumar)wedding and had performed such a long journey after a long time, so surprised to see multi storied flats in Noida. She returned from there and **went away forever in the next month i.e., on 23rd February2020.**

Her memories will remain till I am alive.

After Sushma Only Baba remais for Grand Children !

Travellings with Sushma / Without Sushma!

Traveled a lot with Sushma.

Although travelled nearby pilgrimages like Shri Mahavir ji went many times , but first long rout journey was performed in 1975, i.e., to Shikharji (Sammedshikhar-Parsnath) alongwith Banaras, Chandrapuri, Sarnath etc. Daily details of that journey are as under . All can take advantage of Vandana just by reading .

In this journey sister-in-law Mrs.Jinendra kumari Jain, I Mr.Vijay swaroop Jain, Mrs.Sushma Jain, Neeraj and Neeru along with sister-in-law's mother, Mrs.Rajmati Jain, sister-in-law's maternal grand father ShriRaj Bahadur Jain (Gahetuwale), sister-in-law's aunt and some others.

16 February 1975 Sunday!

It is said that there is no happiness as at home, but sometimes it is felt to go out of the house for sometime. Opportunity to take LFC from Bank was there, so the idea of going got matured.On one side where bank leaves and advance for LFC got approved much sooner than expected, no proper schedule could be decided and due to this could not make reservation of seats in advance.

The leaves were approved from 16th February, which got extended from 17th February and programmed to start from Tundla by Dak Gari train on 16th February which changed to go by TOOFAN EXPRESS train from Agra.

When we reached the platform with ticket, it came to know that either we would not get a place in the train or even if got, would not be able to reach Mughalsarai ,properly. However on making enquiries with collegues it was found that TTs on the train are always to get our problems resolved at some Money.This information made us comfortable .

Well the train arrived and the porter's sympathetic greed resulted in the collusion of him and the owner of the bogie (TT) to get 2 more berths and the journey started well.

When one has to move away from those whose proximity in daily life sometimes seems distasteful due to ideological differences or other reasons, all differences remain aside and a painful tinge of disconnection begins to rise in the heart.

Something similar happened at the station. Pankaj, my niece who is affectionate to me and who had been insisting on going with me for last many days, when he started returning with a sad face, there was moisture in eyes.

Tundla, Etawah, Kanpur station left and the destination started approaching while a TT came ,as the owner and once again we got the opportunity to serve again. A couple from Etawah who might not have been married and could be called as Laila- Majnu or Chintu - Bobby came to our compartment and had a lot of fun. Their conversation revealed that they were both in a college in Kanpur. They went Agra and were returning after visiting the Taj Mahal . Both were hostellers, so the question of taking permission of their parents does not arise because India is free and in this free country, parents have complete freedom to give birth to children .And children have given complete freedom to spoil their future by their parents because they do not have the time to take care of the children and therefore send them to the hostel, where the restrictions of any thing ends.

After Allahabad and small stations reached Mughalsarai . From here we had to change the train and so two porters were called and got the luggage unloaded. I came to know that Sealdah Express train is arriving and we had to travel by this train only.Ther was crowd in the train which got decreased on some stations and got incresed so much before our destination station "Parasnath" that we had unload the luggage through windows.

17-2-1975 Monday !

Today around 10:00 AM, Ishree stayed in Dharamsala at Isharee. After taking bath there, visited the temple and had breakfast. Yesterday was fast on Sunday and because of not taking salt, food with pickles seemed very tasty. After taking meals, packed the luggage , shifted on the bus for Madhuban (Shikharji) and started the journey.

Asked the porter to bring tea before leaving, who brought tea in a kettle and brought very small clay cups, which were one-fourth the volume of the tea cup. Price 40 paise per cup. I was surprised at first But a female passenger told that the price of milk here is ? 6 per liter.

The mini bus whose fare was ? 10 per passenger left from Isri around 12:00 hrs. The fare was collected from the passengers but no ticket or receipt was given even on demand. A sweet named Ram Dana which was very light weight and sweet to eat. On the way, forests full of different types of trees and plants were visible, seeing that the thought came to mind that how vast would be the forest area of this country, where a small part there are innumerable trees and plants.

Reached Madhuban around 2:00 PM. Got the goods from the porters to be kept in the pandal and traced the people who had come earlier and staying in a cottage.Reached there and kept belongings. Had a light breakfast and slept.

After taking meals in the evening, went to the temples. Visited the temple of Terapanthi Kothi, which is very beautiful and there are 13 altars(Vedis) and highly sculpted images.

After darshan and aarti, went to the temple of Bispanthi Kothi, this temple is also very attractive and it has statues in 11 altars.

After returning from here, soon fell asleep due to fatigue. It was decided to go for Vandana in the morning.

18.2 .1975 Tuesday!

Woke up at 2:30 in the morning and came to know that very cold wind is blowing. Due to the ill-health of some collegues, the program of Vandana had to be postponed. Somebody took the Utensil,in which milk was kept for Neeru ,to take a bath. I went to the market and fed milk at the rate of ? 6 per liter, in which at least half the water was. On asking the shopkeeper, who was a Jain, it was found that the price has been increased due to the fair.

It is sad to see how the tendency of exploitation and dishonesty has increased among the traders in the country who, in the pursuit of collecting money, forgetting justice and injustice, collect arbitrary money from the public, that too at pilgrimage places.

After taking a bath, visited the Terapanthi temples and returned to the room and had breakfast and then visited the Bispanthi temples and the Terapanthi Chaubisi temple, which has a magnanimous statue of Bahubali. After seeing both the temples of Shvetambara society, which are beautiful, made a program to go to vandana in the morning and slept.

19. 2 .1975 Wednesday!

Statue of Acharya Shree !08 Shree Vimal Sagar Ji !

At present, in the first phase of starting Tirtha Vandana, all get blessings for worship by lighting a lamp at the tomb of Param Pujya Acharya Shri 108 Shri Vimal Sagar ji Maharaj and also offering the lamp on completion of Vandana!

Woke up at 2:30 this morning and left for Vandana at 3:15 AM Climbing the mountain ,on foot seemed a bit strange ,but it was also a pleasure to climb alongwith many other travelers and companions. We went ahead through different turns. The surrounding forest was full of different types of trees and plants. When the steep climb started, I felt breathless. I had to speed up my walk a little further, leaving most of my friends behind. The climbing became more difficult . Although the weather was cold and the wind was blowing Still the vest was sweaty. After about an hour we reached Gandharva Nala. There is no question of drinking tea before Vandana ,so continued and subsequntly reache Sheetal Nala .

From here two ways are there , one for the Tonk of Gautam Swamiji and the other for the "Swarna Bhadra" koot of Shri Parshvanath. It is said that no impure person can succeed in moving beyond the limit of the Sheetal Nala. If some kind of impurity arises after reaching ahead, then disturbances like storm is inevitable on the mountain.

After climbing for about 3 hours, when I reached the first tonk of Shri Gautam Gandhar ji's at 6:00,I got a very good feeling. The blowing wind was too cold so there was a desire to wear something. On the other side There is tonk (Gyan Dhar Koot) of Shree 1008 Shree Kunth Nath ji.

The sun was trying to break through the dark sky and shined. The sky was looking very beautiful due to the redness of the morning. After offering darshan and offering Arghya to both the tonks, we proceeded for the darshan of other tonks. Offering darshan and Arghya to the four tonks of Shri Naminath (Mitradhar Koot), Shri Arnath (Natak Koot), Shri Mallinath (Sambal Koot) and Shri Shreyansnath Ji (Sankul Koot) reached on the tonk of Shri Pushpdant ji (Suprabh Koot)which is at considerable height .

Descend from here and offering Arghya to Shri Padma Prabhu Ji (Mohan Koot) and Shri Munisuvrat Nath Ji (Nirjar Koot) and then proceed to the tonk of Lord Chandraprabhu Ji (Lalit Koot) which is quite far and also at a height.

After returning from there, reached the feet of Lord Shri Adinath ji who was far away and at a very high altitude. From there, at a short distance, had darshan of Shri Sheetalnath ji (Vidyutbar Koot) and Shri Anant Nath ji (Swayambhu Koot) and offered prayer and Arghya. After descending on Shri Sambhavnath ji's (Dhaval Koot) and then on Vasupujya Bhagwan's feet, Shri Abhinandan Nath (Anand Koot). It is famous for the fact that monkeys must definitely be there at this tonk. From here got down to the Jal Mandir. There is a temple of Shwetambar community which is often closed and opens only in the evening as they go for Vandana in the evening. Coins were shining in the water tank built around the Jal Mandir, which was showing the faith of the people. Arrived via (Kundaprabhu Koot) at the feet of Lord Mahavir. from where, after seeing Shri Suparshvanath ji's

(Prabhas koot) and Shri Vimalnath ji's (Subir koot), reached Shri Ajitnath ji's (Subir koot)via Shri Ajitnath ji's (Siddhavarkoot), Lord Neminath feet and finally after crossing a great distance and height, finally to worship at Shri Parshwnath Bhagwan's (Swarnabhadra Koot) and performed poojan and aarti by lighting a lamp.There are Charan (feet) at two places and got Darshan of both .

This was the last stop of the journey and from here one has to start returning.

First arrived at the guest house (Dak Bungalow) took tea. Though taxis are available from here but at high fare. After getting down from the bungalow walked a long distance upto Sheetal Nala. Here too the tea shop has opened but kept on going. Tea and breakfast were arranged by the committee. People from both sides of Bispanthi and Terapanthi started pulling for their own for breakfast. There they had breakfast of Sev (gram flour), boondi laddoos and tea .

Again covered a great distance and looking at different types of trees and plants kept mooving. There were also some shortcuts which covered the distance in less time.

Forest at Sammed Shikharji Parvat !

During the visit of Shri Sammed Shikharji, there was a huge forests on the way.
One thing was astonishing that not a single creature like lion,tiger was seen in such a huge forest. Otherwise it is inevitable to find lions etc. in suchforests. It is probably a miracle that many travelers start at night without proper lighting arrangements. There are very narrow roads. But there are no accidents.

Another thing which was visible here is poverty. On one hand there are people in the country for whom new ways of spending money are thought, on the other hand there are more number of people who are unable to even get enough food. And for some money, they keep spreading their bags in front of others.

While coming down from the mountain, seeing the beggars from place to place, we feel sorrow.

About 300 beggars were found in the entire unloading, people of all ages children, men and women from the age of 6 years to 70 years, wer there but the number of children was the highest.

20.02.1975 Thursday!

Woke up very late this morningand went to temple. Returned to have breakfast and then slept. Woke up in the evening and reached at pandal which was being built for the Panchkalyanak festival and was very spacious and attractive.

21.02. 1975 Friday!

Today we again went for Vandana. Neeru and Neeraj were with the docks and Sushma in Doli. All others on foot. Today's worship took a lot of time as one had to walk slowly along with all the people.

When only three tonks remained, I had to arrange doli for sister Mrs. Maina Devi Jain because she was very much tired and was not feeling well. I came down around 3:00 PM . On returning, sister's health deteriorated and consulted two doctors and treatment arranged.

22.02.1975 Saturday!

Woke up , took a bath and went to the pandal after worship.

23.02.1975 Sunday!

Today I was scheduled to go for Vandana, but did not go due to bad weather. After bathing in Terapanthi temple, I did Abhishek and recited Shri Sammed Shikhar Path in Chaubisi temple.

24.2.1975 Monday!

Went for the third Vandana today. I walked slowly due to knee pain since beginning and could return at 1:30 PM. Today was Moksha Kalyanak.

25.02.1975 Tuesday!

This morning, after taking a bath, having darshan and having food, bought some herbs from the market and accounted for milk etc. Today, at the time of Abhishek, I visited Shri 105 Parshwanath and Shri 105 Vishram Mata ji and darshan idols of their temple . I had the privilege of seeing and doing the cleaning.

26.02.1975 Wednesday!

Woke up in the morning and prayed on the power rock(Pawar Shila). From there 2-3 Tonk's are visible. Today there was a program to go to Giridih but remained in Madhuban till 4:00 in the evening. After visiting the temples, depart for Giridih Bus Stand at 4:00 PM. At 5:30, the bus got available which was to go to Ara, but due to the excessive ride of Giridih, the in-charge asked to take that bus to Giridih and left. When the luggage was placed in the bus, the driver of the bus said that he Won't take the bus to Giridih. After about 1 hour of trouble another bus arrived and reached Giridih at 7:00. Hardly found a place in Dharamsala. Opened the bed and rested. Went to the temple again. There are three vedies in the temple which are quite delightful. First, Shri Bahubali Bhagwan's second Shri Parasnath in the form of Bhagwan and one more. After that I went to the market. Got milk at cheaper rate than Shikharji. Took some other items for meals and came back .

27.02 .1975 Thursday!

In the morning performed Abhishek and worship and on returning went to another temple. From there a car goes to Deoghar and from Deoghar one has to go to Bossi by bus or taxi. But after not getting the car till evening, we came back.

28 .02.1975 Friday !

Today reached Bosi by bus ,directly. There is a Jain temple here which is well carved. There is an altar on which there is a grand stone idol of Moolnayak Shri Vasupujya Bhagwan , one idol of Shri Adinath ji's Khadgasan and one of Shri Vasupujya Bhagwan. After having darshan took food and went to sleep after aarti in the evening. Arrange a programme to go to the mountain next morning.

1.03. 1975 Saturday!

Waking up in the morning and after Prakshal, went to the mountain by rickshaw. From here, Mandargiri is about 2 miles and about 1 mile to mountain. Climbing was a pleasurable . There are three tonks Lord Shri Vasupujya's feet established in all three .We felt relaxed.

Sad to see a number of beggars on the way back. The whole Vandana is about 3 hours. Returned to take meals and tied the bed to come to station and buy tickets to Bhagalpur. The train reached about 45 minutes late and remained at the station for half an hour. Reached Bhagalpur at 3:30, seeing various scenic views on the way. Reached Jain Dharamshala by rickshaw but due to overcrowding, no room was found vacant. So had to stay in the verandah. In the evening, the goods were kept in the gardener's room and went to the market for a walk. There is a chaityalaya in the street .

2.03.1975 Sunday!

Waking up around 4:00 AM and left for Champapur (Nathnagar). There are 2 temples in Champapur. One is very ancient and the other is new . The first temple has only one altar and the other there are seven altars , in which apart from the idol of Moolnayak Shri Bhagwan Vasupujya, there are many attractive and evocative idols.

On moving to Nawada the Passenger train was late and passed on. But people told that the next train (Vardhman Express) will be better to go to Nawada. That train also arrived late by 1 hour 30 minutes and left Bhagalpur at 3:30. Going through different stations reached the Mule Junction, where the train was parked for a long time. The passengers sitting in the coaches were called in the same compartment and made candles, matches and torches. Put out of the boxes because the people of the area have fully used their freedom and all the things like bulb switches etc. have been taken out from all the coaches of this train. Train moooved very slowly and reached at 9:30 PM to Nawada station. The goods were put in the rickshaw and reached the Jain temple which was inside the Dharamsala. Had to stay there in the verandah. There is only one altar in the temple. Although the mosquitoes of Bihar are famous, but the mosquitoes here welcomed us and healed the ears with its melodious music at night and the bodies with its mouth.

3.03.1975 Monday !

Woke up in the morning and left for Pavapur by taxi. On the way saw Gudava ji from where Gautam Gandhara ji got salvation. There are 2 temples. One has an altar and in other feet of Tirthankaras and Gautam Swami are there as also the feet of Digambara Lord Parshvanath and 2 Shwetambar idols. After visiting here, boarded the taxi and reached Pavapur Siddha Kshetra. Jal Mandir was visible from a far, around which there is a huge pond. After reaching the temple, took bath in the room and performed poojan/Prakshala. The temple is very beautiful. On the ground floor ther are majestic statues of Lord Mahavir as well as other magnificent idols. There are four chaityalayas on the first floor which also have very beautiful idols and steps are installed. From here we went to the Jal Mandir from where Lord Mahavira had attained salvation. In the temple, which is very beautiful, the feet of Lord Mahavir are established. Worshiped here too. Returned ,took meals and slept. Waking up at 5:00 in the evening, went to see the Shvetambar temple and returned. Came back after performing aarti at the Jal Mandir .

4.03. 1975 Tuesday!

In the morning, after completing bath etc., worshiped /Prakshal and after having lunch, left for Rajgrihi from Pavapur. First went to Kundalpur, which is the birthplace of Lord Mahavir ji. Came and proceeded to see the museum and the old ruins. Bought Khaja from Selava village and reached Rajgrihi in the evening. After keeping the belongings in the room, reached the temple and made a program to go for Vandana in the morning.

5 March 1975 Wednesday !

Waking up in the morning went for Vandana. The doli was found at high fare because the doli lifters were on strike. For Rs26.25 per doli twodoli's and one tonga arranged. There are 5 mountains. There are stairs to go to each. Total steps are about 4000 . While going to the mountain, we got hot water pools. Naturally hot water, which is said to be sulfur water is very beneficial for the body and stomach. Due to lack of time, could not make a programme to stay for long time. There are 5 tonks on the first mountain. Four of the Digambar and one of the Shvetambar . From there the road to the second mountain is very rough and full of stones. The Doli people are able to take it with a lot of care,hard work and pain. Descending from here the stairs to the third mountainwhich are also at distance. After coming down from this mountain, had breakfast, which was arranged by the committee . After breakfast, went to the fourth mountain. There is Buddha Temple , which was built by Japan. reached there by trolley/ropeway. The temple has 4 statues of Gautam Buddha in 4 forms. The idols had gilded water on them. Unique and attractive sculptures attract travelers towards themselves. In a nearby room, a Buddhist monk continues to play the drums and recite the peace mantra, possibly in Japanese. On the way back, the trolley stopped in the middle due to electicity failure. Deep down hills were visible. Reached the mountain and from there again on the fifth mountain. Worshiped there and returned and bathed in the hot water pool. Returning from there, came to Dharamsala and had meals.

6.03.1975 Thursday !

Woke up early and packed the luggage as the train was at 6:40. But on reaching the station, the train started running. The train got stopped with a lot of difficulty and boarded . The train stoppage at Gulzarbagh station was for 2 minutes. Some milkmen had put containers ,full of milk ,near the door in such a way that there was a lot of difficulty in getting out. Some luggage remained inside and the train started. I had to jump with luggage at the station causing injury to my leg.This is the place of nirvana of Seth Sudarshan.

7.03.1975 Friday !

Waking up in the morning and pouring salt mixed hot water on the feet, which gave some relief, then went out to visit the temples, after visiting some of the temples , went to visit the temples built in the ashram located at Dharupur. There are 4 temples. Attractive and peace giver Lord Bahubali is seated, along with many other Gods. I went to "Adinath Blind Vidyalaya" where the teacher told us that after losing eyes, man got physically distressed .He suffered more because of neglectful behavior of the society. Small handicrafts making units like towels / bags are there. After visiting Dharamsala, reached station and took tickets for Banaras. The train "Bareilly", which left at 5:00 in the evening, reached Banaras at 10:00 in the night. Stayed in Bihari Lal Dharamsala.

8.03.1975 Saturday!

After morning darshan took breakfast and went to visit various temples by taxi at 12:00. In the evening, around 3:00 PM, reached Chandrapuri which is 25 km away. And there had been Gyan Kalyanak. The festival of Kalyanak was being celebrated, so the temple was very crowded. There is also a Buddhist temple here which has an attractive statue of Lord Buddha. After coming back and having food, we went to the market to buy some toys.

9.03.1975 Sunday !

Woke up in the morning and took a boy with whom visited 3 nearby temples. After returning, started preparing to pack up. In the evening, around 3:00 PM, left for the station. From here to Tundla we had to go by Upper India train, in which a bogie is attached from here. I got a comfortable place in it and, just two and a half hours late Upper India, reached at 9:45 in the night and reached Etawah at 8:00 AM.

10.03.1975 Monday!

Today at 8:00 AM, Sister Maina Devi Jain was at Etawah and proceeded. Reached Tundla and then Agra.This was the good end of big journey.

Shri Sammed Shikharji again visited in 1997 from 7th August to 13th August (on the occasion of joining time in Aligarh City).

On August 7.1997 departed from Agra Fort station at 6:15 a.m. from Jodhpur Howrah to Shri Sammed Shikharji and landed at Shri Parasnath station at 11:30 p.m. Returned back at 4:12 AM on 12th August 1997 by

Howrah Jodhpur Express and reached Agra at 9:30 PM.

First time after Sushma- visit of Shri Sammed Shikharji from 17.12.2021 to 23.12.2021

17.12.2021 Friday !

Today was the programme to go to Shri Sammed Shikharji's , from Tundla by Poorva Express at 8:40. Arrived at Tundla station at 8:00. Mr. Jinesh Kumar, Vineeta ,Mr. Amit, Neeru, Muskaan, Rishabh, were also to go by the same train from Delhi. All of them came in my coach and the conversation continued. Their coach was after four to five bogies. Today was the fast of Chaturdashi. I fell asleep early.

One employee in health department in Ghazipur and returning from Agra after training was praising Yogi and Modi a lot. What they had done is commendable. He told that if he used to come for training earlier, it became only passing time. Now he was satisfied by training. He told that the government is spending so much money on the treatment of poor that the last stage patient of TV, an injection comes to about ? 500000, that too is provided free of cost.

18 12 2021 Saturday !

Today at 11:00 AM we got down at Parasnath station and came out and left for Madhuban (Shikhar ji) by minibus. Arrived at Siddhayatan after about 45 minutes. Mr. Mishra ji (Sea Tv official) was there with keys of rooms . All got shifted to rooms and after taking baths had darshan in the temple. Arrived at the restaurant. Today was Saturday, so oil was not to be consumed. Ritu had cooked food from Agra.

In the evening reached at Gunayatan, to Maharaj Shri 108 Praman Sagar ji and had darshan and after sitting in "Shanka Samadhan", a programme of devotional evening was organized by Jinvani channel in which many artists participated. Jinvani's team had already reached there.

19 12 2021 Sunday !

Today, in Gunayatan, Neeraj got bid for Shanti Dhara for three lakh and Maharaj ji cited Large Shanti Dhara(of 1008 mantras). The touch by Maharaj Shri on my head was thrilled. Neeraj also announced a donation for 50% discount on Maharaj's literature and also bid for the "Gandhar Valaya" legislation to be held in Gunayatan temple from 11:00 AM. The legislation ended at 1:00 PM and after that, at 2:30, the programmme of change of Maharaj Shree's PICHHI began. Prior to the PICHHI PARIVARTAN, a documentary prepared by Jinvani channel (which was suitable for the time

,in which Indra from heaven collects PICHHI from Acharya Shri 108 Shree Vidya Sagar Ji for Maharaj Shri 108 Praman Sagar ji and bring it to Gunayatan) was shown ,which everyone liked very much.

Reached Gunayatan in the evening and after that went to the market. Tonight there was a programmefor Vandana . Those who had to go by the dolis, booked the dolis.

20 December 2021 Monday!

At about 3:00 PM, came from Siddhayatan to Terapanthi Kothi, took Doli and started Vandana. It was very cold. I wanted to go to Vandana in Dhoti dupatta but Neeru and others refused and I was completely ready with clothes, socks and hand glubsbut still felt severe cold in my feet.

Vandana started by lighting a lamp at the samadhi of Acharya Shri 108 Vimal Sagar ji Maharaj and seeking blessings.

On the way, Muskaan also took the doli because she was unable to walk . We reached the first "Gandhar Tonk" at around 7:00 PM and offered samagri after having darshan . Neeru lit the lamp by lighting camphor. She lit the lamps almost on all the tonks. I should also took deepaks and camphor. I had carried a dhoti dupatta and innerwear with me in a bag, thinking that I would do abhishek in the temple of Chopra Kund. Upon reaching there, regretted seeing the condition where the temple was located. There was a filth inside and outside and Gods were locked . It was a very painful situation.

Came down from the mountain around 5:30 and went straight to the breakfast table at Terapanthi Kothi.

The best journey was done by Neeraj, Sonal, Shri Pramod ji (Neeraj's father-in-law), Gungun and Gracy. They were able to come down at about 8:00, that too with the helpof two motorcyclists.

On 20.12.2021 at Shri Chandraprabhu talk of Shri Sammed Shikharji with eldest daughter Smt. Neeru Jain!

21st December 2021!

Woke up this morning at 5:30 AM. Everyone was sleeping. Before waking them up, I thought of their being tired so didn't ask to wake up. Suddenly at 6:30, Neeraj's voice heard and immediately started towards Terapanthi Kothi for Abhishek. The bid of Shanti dhara over Moolnayak Bhagwan 1008 Shri Pushpdant ji was taken by another person, joined him and the Aryaka Mataji, sitting on the field did a favour for making Shanti Dhara over

Bhagwan 1008 Shri Parshvanath ji.

Today Shri Jinesh Kumar, Vinita, Shri Pramod ji went back by Rajdhani Express. In the afternoon, visited Bispanthi Kothi and in the evening had darshan of Antarmana Muni Shri 108 Shri Prasanna Sagar Ji Maharaj. Maharaj Shri on 567 days fasts (from 21st July 2021 to 23 January 2023) and will fast for 496 days and take food only 61 days.

He is doing penance alone in a room on the upper floor and at 6:30 in the evening when the devotees gather for the aarti below, he opens the window for 2 minutes and offers blessings and the window gets closed.

22 December 2021!

This morning after Abhishek Shantidhara at Siddhayatan Chaityalaya, also went to Terapanthi Kothi and after returning made preparations to return after breakfast. Leaving Madhuban at around 11:30, boarded the train from Parasnath station and landed at Tundla on 23 December 2021 at around 3:00 AM and From there came back to Agra.

In a short time memorable journey performed , **full credit goes to Neeraj.**

Unfulfilled Dreams Of Sushma !

After Sushma's departure, I have nothing but memories of her. I am thinking that I should fulfill the promises made to her before my leaving, in which the construction of the Jain temple was the main. Apart from this, I want to do something for the service of animals and birds, through Gaushala and Birds nests.

Although she installed idols of GOD (Tirthankars) in few temples during her living, including Lord Chandraprabhu Temple Firozabad, Ahikshetra Temple (Ramnagar) and some other temples, whose names I do not remember. but her major wish was **building a Jain temple and insaling Idol of God in it,** which could not be built during her lifetime. Although the **land for the temple has been arranged in a colony,** at Agra, unfortunately construction of the temple could not be started during her lifetime. I hope I can fulfill her dream durin my life.

Om ! Sweet Om !

Jai Jinendra!

Think over it SERIOUSLY !

Should we consider ourselves vegetarian , if we :

-Visit restaurants/hotels where non veg is prepared/ served

-Use BONE China crockery

-Attention marriages/other functions arranged in Non Veg Hotels

-Eat and serve pastries/cakes etc without confirming that these are eggless or not .

Be True Vegetarian proudly !

Sushma jain -writing Namokar Mantra !

S M D J M Charitable Trust

Humble invitation!

**Contact us to become a Trustee or Associate in the Trust.
Join for social service, animal service, poor service!
The donation given is tax free under section 80G of Income
Tax.
Smt. Mahadevi Jain Memorial Charitable Trust
S M D J M Charitable Trust**

PAN : AASTS5416N
Contact :8191099999, 9319773237
email : smdjmc@gmail.com
"Saubhagya", 118, Manas Nagar, Shahganj, Agra-282010 (Uttar Pradesh-India)
URN (80 G) - AASTS5416NF20226
Efforts are being made by the Trust to start the following services:
1. Cooperation of various cowsheds / roaming cows, straw / fodder etc. to animals for cow service.
2. Arrangement of food / clothes etc. for poor / helpless persons / widows.
3. Arrangement of fees / books for poor and deserving students.
4. Land is being seen for Gaushala and Veterinary Hospital.
5.Looking for space for poor children's school.

Feed Straw Animals !